Business is Personal

A blueprint for unlocking meaning at work

By Corrie J Block, PhD, DBA

Business is Personal
Copyright © 2021 By Corrie J Block, PhD, DBA
First published in 2021

Print: 978-1-922456-40-3
E-book: 978-1-922456-41-0
Hardback: 978-1-922456-39-7

All rights reserved. No part of this book may be reproduced, stored in a retrieval system, or transmitted by any means (electronic, mechanical, photocopying, recording, or otherwise) without written permission from the author.

Because of the dynamic nature of the Internet, any web addresses or links contained in this book may have changed since publication and may no longer be valid. The information in this book is based on the author's experiences and opinions. The views expressed in this book are solely those of the author and do not necessarily reflect the views of the publisher; the publisher hereby disclaims any responsibility for them.

The author of this book does not dispense any form of medical, legal, financial, or technical advice either directly or indirectly. The intent of the author is solely to provide information of a general nature to help you in your quest for personal development and growth. In the event you use any of the information in this book, the author and the publisher assume no responsibility for your actions. If any form of expert assistance is required, the services of a competent professional should be sought.

Publishing information
Publishing, design, and production facilitated by Passionpreneur Publishing, A division of Passionpreneur Organization Pty Ltd, ABN: 48640637529

www.PassionpreneurPublishing.com
Melbourne, VIC | Australia

Table of Contents

Dedication — iv
Foreword — v
Introduction — 1

CHAPTER 1: Business is Personal — 9
CHAPTER 2: Personal Words are Meaningful — 31
CHAPTER 3: Corporate Words are Meaningful — 47
CHAPTER 4: Mutual Vision: Why you're in your role — 71
CHAPTER 5: Mutual Mission: How we're getting it done — 101
CHAPTER 6: Mutual Values: Who we are in community — 133
CHAPTER 7: Mutual Goals: What we are accomplishing together — 157

Appendix A: Values List — 193
Bibliography — 201

Dedication

For my son, Gabriel.

As you journey through your career, never lose sight of those to your right and left, your teammates at work, your economic tribe whose efforts are helping you meet your personal goals. You need them as much as they need you. Be connected. Be empathetic. You deserve their respect, and they deserve your best performance.

May you always be treated, and treat others, as humans and not resources. And may your work make you proud of yourself. I am certainly proud of you.

Foreword

By James (a significant character in this book)

You will, hopefully, be able to connect with all sections in this book and identify yourself with the individuals, their thought processes, and in some cases, obstacles that have impacted them. You will witness how they have grown and adapted to an ever-changing platform, both at home and work.

I am in my late 40s, a professional and expert in my chosen field. I have attended some of Dr. Corrie's programs and read about the various subjects that he has introduced me to. The most important of them is probably the one that surrounds my Vision, Mission, Values, and Goals (VMV&Gs) and how I have adapted (sometimes not even realizing it) to drive my professional career and family life forward under the direction and targets I deemed important for my family and me.

In reality, I have changed over the years as situations around me changed, the biggest of which was when I had a family to care for. My VMV&Gs immediately changed, and what was important to me months earlier, was now insignificant as new things drove me forward. As individuals, I firmly believe, we are all constantly changing and adapting. However, the more successful among us, think about that change and plan for it. Having the ability to look ahead and set personal goals that align to my Vision is something that I am now clear about, thanks to Dr Corrie. It had always been there, but he drew it out and showed me the interrelation between my professional and family lives. Both, I might add, are now far stronger and structured, and I feel part of a committed community.

I am happy at home and at work, and always see the positive as opposed to the negative. I didn't realize it some years ago, but my personal VMV&Gs have taken me to the role I now have, and aligned me to my company's VMV&Gs, closer than I thought possible. As humans, we will always come across stones in the journey, but the reality is, provided you commit to and are confident of what you seek, it is easy to climb over the obstacles and get back onto the right path. Trust in your community, as you deserve to be there.

I urge you to follow the book from start to finish – take your time, think about what matters and put down on paper honest answers to the questions you are about to be asked. I am 8 kgs lighter now (that will make more sense later on in the book) but it remains a Goal I constantly have to work for. The dopamine hit, however, is worth it. Finally, not many people know this but I love a bit of sci-fi, and as Agent Scully of X-Files fame says, "The truth is out there." So be honest with yourself and you will get far more out of this book than you think.

Introduction

"Careers are a jungle gym, not a ladder."

– Sheryl Sandberg

If you could live a more meaningful life without making any major changes to it, would you want that?

My wife and I recently took a trip to the Maldives. It's a beautiful country made up of hundreds of tiny island resorts. Our resort was graced by pristine blue waters, beaches that wrapped around the entire facility, and the whole cast of *Finding Nemo* out among the corals every day, waving out to us! But the award-winning differentiator for me was a Sri Lankan concierge named Taj.

Taj was in his late 20s. Tall and thin, his white teeth shone like the Cheshire cat against his dark skin. When we first reached the resort, he greeted us, informed us of where we'd be staying, and told us that he could help with arranging activities, spa sessions, or special meals for us. Then, he dropped us off at our beach villa, and vanished. But vanishing wasn't his special gift; appearing out of the blue was.

For the next five days, at the most random and yet opportune times, Taj would uncannily materialize. At the pool, the snack bar, walking past the main restaurant, you name it. We would suddenly look up, and there he was, offering to book a restaurant for dinner, or a paddleboard for the following morning. One of those days, we were walking around the whole island, which took about 90 minutes. We were at the far end of the island, as far away from our villa as we could get, when suddenly, out from a nearby footpath, popped up Taj, sporting a huge grin.

"Hello, Dr. & Mrs. Block, how are you today?"

"Hi Taj, where did you come from?"

"I was nearby and wanted to see if you would like to take advantage of some spa time tomorrow, before it's all booked up."

Which, of course, we did. It was incredible, borderline magical, how he would know what we wanted before we wanted it, and appear quite from nowhere to make sure we could get it.

You know those rare moments when you interact with someone whose job is incredibly complex, and yet, when you watch them do it, it appears effortless to them? People who are so one with work that their job doesn't seem like much of a job at all? That was Taj.

Introduction

When we departed, Taj walked us out to the plane, helped us get seated, and then, as we took off from the water with the resort on our right, there he stood. He stayed on the dock, waving to us until we were out of sight. He was a miracle. It was clear to me that he found a great deal of meaning in his work, and that his work was a large part of his meaningful life.

You deserve to live a meaningful life like that, and that's what I'm offering through this book. This book is primarily a guide to helping you discover meaning at work through the lens of your personal vision, mission, values, and goals. Be careful though, because if you read on, you are unlikely to ever view your career in the same way again.

♦ ♦ ♦

In 2011, *Harvard Business Review* suggested that "meaning is the new money."[1] This has never been truer than it is now. A decade of separate research studies reveal that, today, 90% of employees will work harder for less money if they are doing work that they find meaningful.[2] The value of meaningful work is growing in importance over time.

---

1 Erickson, T, 'Meaning Is the New Money'. Retrieved December 15, 2019, from https://hbr.org/2011/03/challenging-our-deeply-held-as

2 Hu, J., & Hirsh, J. B. (2017). *Accepting Lower Salaries for Meaningful Work.* Frontiers in Psychology, 8.

So, given the choice, you'd most likely do a meaningful job for less money if you could. But what if you didn't have to change jobs to find that meaning? What if you already had the tools you needed, but just didn't know how to use them? What value would be in it for you to find a higher quality of life without changing it?

That was the case for James, whom you'll meet in Chapter 4. He's a family man in his early 40s. Wife, kids, nice home in the suburbs, and a decent job. For the first time in his life, in early 2019, James was able to articulate his personal vision, mission, values, and goals. Now that's not all that unique, since there are already a dozen books on the self-help shelf on articulating your life purpose. What James needed was to take the next step toward using those words to find meaning at work.

Personal life statements are common, but what was truly new for James, and may be a blessing for you, were the skills to articulate why he had chosen his particular career path and ended up in his current job. It wasn't an accident. It was a series of deliberate choices based on his own character. He chose a specific role in a specific community. And that community chose James for that specific role. Understanding how that happens and being able to see it in black and white was empowering for James. It added meaning to his life. He didn't need to change his job to find that meaning — he only needed a new point of view and a little coaching.

Do you feel disconnected at work? Do you feel like you are working a job because you are obligated to? Do you feel that

Introduction

you hate your job? Your boss? Your co-workers? Do you feel like you're living two separate lives, one at work and one outside? If so, then it's time to discover the meaning in what you're doing.

Meaninglessness at work is like a cancer that can grow unseen in your heart over time, slowly reducing the quality of your life, until one day, the cancer metastasizes: you wake up and hate your job. But it's never "just a job", is it? It's half of your life. And when people hate half of their lives, well, that's just not acceptable to me. You deserve to know with great clarity why you are in the job you're in. And you deserve to connect meaningfully and passionately with the work you are already doing.

So, imagine, by the end of this simple book, you will have a much clearer understanding of your vision, mission, values, and goals, and how your current job role fits into a life strategy that you have been executing for years already. Imagine that you will also have tools for building that level of meaning into the lives of colleagues you have partnered with and care for, both in and out of your current organization.

This book is for people like James, who may or may not have great clarity on their life purpose, and how their current jobs connect with that purpose. It's also for managers and leaders in organizations who want a new set of tools for building meaningfulness into the lives of their team members. Human resource professionals will also certainly benefit from one of the absolute best practices for employee engagement in these tools – so they can be more intentional about how to create meaning in their corporate communities.

On a practical note, one of the things this book does is to reduce to a minimum, the number of inputs you will need from other people. You shouldn't need a lot of outside input to go through this book.

Another thing this book does is to focus on your usage of words. We all know intrinsically how meaningful words can be, but very few of us seem to be able to make them work powerfully for ourselves. Choosing words well and connecting with them can bring life and light into your career.

It's only fair to warn you that this is not a feel-good book. You will not feel the emotional hand-holding that you might get in other books. There won't be anyone listening to all of your woes, and telling you that you can rise above your current circumstances, if you just meditate more and eat better. There will be no new chants or mantras. And this material will move well beyond telling you that positivity is the key to changing your life.

This is an educational book, and your life is its primary target. It's a workbook, and you'll have to do some writing along the way. Actually, the odds are pretty good that you've been gifted this book by a kind and caring manager or leader in your life, so the two of you can talk later about how you've ended up in your current role, and why it's valuable for you to remain engaged in your organization.

Introduction

This material is based on real research, spanning two decades, thirty countries, and more than a hundred and fifty companies. It's arranged in two parts. Chapters 1 through 3 outline the background and reasoning behind my approach to using meaningful words in human communities as a tool for tapping into a meaningful life. Chapters 4 through 7 are geared toward helping you clarify the meaningful words that have been governing your life so far, and re-articulating them for you to make more meaningful decisions in the future.

Throughout the book, we will dance between the language of individuals and organizations, because, as it will be made clear in Chapters 1 and 2, there is no individual without an organization, and there is no organization without the individual. Tens of thousands of years of human evolution have fused the two. Humans have evolved and adapted to survive and reproduce, and our best resource for doing both is our community. So, the lines separating individual and community (organization) will blur in this book, as they have blurred in human lives since the beginning of recorded history.

I've guided thousands of corporate clients on this journey to finding meaning at work. I've helped managers and leaders in more than 150 companies, across 30 different countries, to complete this process over the last 25 years. From CEOs and Board Chairpersons to entry level managers, I've seen the impact of this journey on both individual lives and organizations as a whole. And I'm excited to be working with you now!

By the end of this journey, you will be able to answer two fundamental questions about your current job:

1. Why am I *here* (and not somewhere else)? and,
2. Why am *I* here (and not someone else)?

But first, let's start with a community event which is a personal favorite of mine, and the environment in which I've had hundreds of these conversations already. Come with me to a backyard barbeque for a moment, I want to introduce you to Ben, and to the power of words.

CHAPTER 1

Business is Personal

It was a beautiful day. The air was clear, and the weather, perfect. A great day for a BBQ. We were a dozen odd people, all hanging out in our friend's backyard on a Friday afternoon for some stories, laughter, sharing of secrets, and the all-important Jack and Coke that I enjoy over ice on days like this. I didn't know most of those around me, so I made an effort to connect. And like most people, I asked the standard questions in typical order:

"What's your name, mate?"

"Ben."

"Where are you from? Wait, U.K.?"

"London, well, just outside of London. You?"

"Canada, originally. But I haven't lived there in more than 20 years. How long have you lived in Dubai?"

"About 10 years, I guess."

"And what do you do?"

"I'm a Project Manager for a construction company."

[pause]

Let's take a step outside of this otherwise simple conversation to reflect on the meaning of these questions and why we ask them like this of each other, almost always in that order.

What's Your Name?

Research has shown that every person's favorite word is their own name. It's our first (and usually last) moniker, the first word that, we learn as babies, belongs entirely to us, and refers almost all the time to us personally. We hang on to that word because it's meaningful. It's how we know we are being called, thought of, remembered, and matter.

It's why Dale Carnegie made remembering peoples' names one of his three rules for *How to Win Friends and Influence People*.[3] We are our names, whether given or chosen, and whether or not it's a nickname, it's how we like to be identified. It's what our mothers and fathers first called us, and so, it's a core linguistic artifact in our personal identity. That's why, it's most often the first question when we meet someone. What's in a name then? Well, you are.

---

3 Carnegie, D. (2009). How to Win Friends and Influence People. *Simon & Schuster.*

Where are You From?

In Dubai, a majority of the population comprises expatriates. So, almost all of us here are really from somewhere else. India, China, Russia, or in my case, Canada. Knowing where someone is from gives us a head start in figuring out their personal culture by narrowing down the field of possibilities to a dominant culture of origin, usually a nation or an ethnic group. This helps inform us on how that person might want to be treated, based on our knowledge and experience of their culture of origin. This is another one of Dale Carnegie's rules — treating people the way they expect to be treated.

How Long Have You Been in Dubai?

Since very few of us hail from Dubai, it helps to know how long another has lived here. The longer it's been, the more they'll be accustomed to the place, and subconsciously, the less they may expect to be treated as they would in their culture of origin. This, again, gives us a clue on how to treat each other.

And What Do You Do?

Anywhere in the world, this question will come up among the first 3-5 questions that one asks upon meeting someone for the first time. This is an important fact. What you do for work is an indication of your social role. Humans are social creatures, and we like to know what the other is doing to participate in society. This helps us to not only know how to treat each other, but also gives us a window into each other's personality, character, life purpose, and dreams. We ask doctors questions that are different from what we'd ask school teachers, accountants, and graphic designers.

So, knowing a little about Ben — that he's from London and has spent the last 10 years in Dubai, and is currently a Project Manager — could help guide the kind of things we might talk about, the kind of jokes he might find funny, and the degree to which his culture of origin might have been tempered by a decade in Dubai. It's a natural foray from here into sports like football (the non-American kind) or cricket, job particulars like management or the construction industry, or topics of entertainment such as whether or not he'd seen Fawlty Towers or Monty Python (both of which I love, by the way). That would have been natural.

But that's not what I did.

About 5 years ago, I decided to start hijacking first-time conversations to make them a little more meaningful. As a practice, I pretty consistently move from here into the two questions I now typically ask next.

[play]

"Are you good at it?"

"My job? As good as the next person, I guess. Work gets done. There are good days, and bad."

"Do you enjoy it?"

"Well, I dunno. It's a job, it's not really who I am."

[pause]

And there it is, my dear Reader. It's for this reason, this very response, that I have written this entire book. For Ben, and for all of those like him who would reply in a similar way to these questions.

Take a minute now and answer those questions for yourself. It won't take long. Just a simple note for later reference:

Are you good at your job?

_____

Do you enjoy it?

_____

Your Job was Your Life

I have noticed that more often than not, in my deviations from typical introductions, my "Do you enjoy it?" question elicits a kind of dispassionate reply which I had not only expected, but felt increasingly responsible for addressing. And to do that, we need to take a short trip down memory lane. I love history to move … are you ready?

Until the Industrial Revolution, humans worked all the time. We didn't have break times for lunch, or off on Saturdays. We rarely got a choice of career, let alone a career change once we were in one. Most humans did what their parents did for work. In fact, in many societies, you would have been known not by your father's name, but by his social role. If born into a family that made horse-drawn carts, your last name would likely have been Cartwright; if your family worked with metal, then you were likely a Smith. Those named Fletcher would have been associated with archery, perhaps the manufacture of arrows. As a Block, I'm probably wearing a name granted by a history of masonry or construction workers.

And our jobs weren't just jobs. They represented who we were in society, the role we played, and the value we added to our tribal, national, or economic communities. There was no division of work from life, because work was life. For the majority of humans, food was scarce, security a luxury, and our survival was contingent on our ability to carry out our social roles well. We were what we did for work. Anything outside of that was leisure, and leisure too, was luxury.

The Industrial Revolution saw the rise of new manufacturing efficiencies. A single company owner could hire all of the available Smiths in the area to work in a single metal factory, or all the local Taylors for a single textile factory. That made the groups of Smiths and Taylors more competitive in a globalizing economy by pooling all of their efforts in mass production. Until the mid-19th century, it was commonplace for a worker to log 100 hours a week in this new kind of coordinated social role. There still wasn't much to "life" outside of work, and we derived meaning and identity from our societal roles. Whatever life there was, it existed primarily within those social roles. It might be depicted a bit like this:

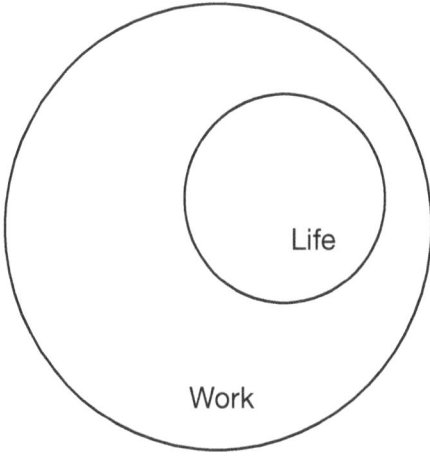

The Beginnings of Life Outside Work

By the mid-19th century, some industries had people working so hard that the employees themselves started to complain about fatigue and lack of rest. So, industrialists started playing around with the work week. A number of Western organizations adopted a 50-hour workweek as a response to unionized labor pressure. This not only led to more non-working time for employees but, to the delight of the owners of these industries, it also fostered higher productivity and higher profits. Well-rested humans performed better work.

By the first half of the 20th century, economists were conducting coordinated research on what made people more efficient as employees. In 1926, Henry Ford was the first to institute the 40-hour work week, effectively dividing the amount of time spent in and out of work in half. This had the dual benefit of producing more profits for Ford out of the new efficiency found in an 8-hour work day, and improving the quality of life for employees who now had time to explore other activities during non-working hours. It was a win-win for industrialists and their employees. In a series of reforms between 1933 and 1939 by U.S. President Franklin D. Roosevelt, the 40-hour week became a national labor policy.

And just like that, we had work-life balance:

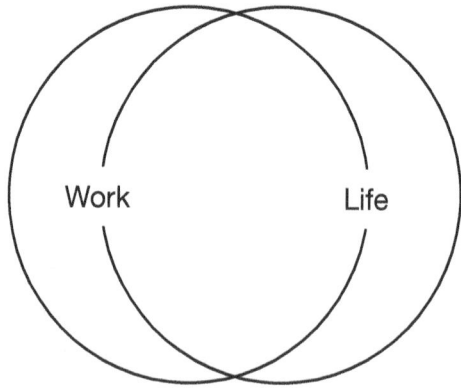

Humans were living more efficiently than ever before. We could perform social roles in economic communities that enabled better food security and general prosperity.

Suddenly, we had time to do things we wanted. We were still primarily known by our work roles, but we also had more time to spend with family, hang out with our friends in the pub, play football in the empty lot down the street, and enjoy a backyard BBQ on the newly created weekend. What a great deal!

Life is Other Than Work

But then, shit hit the fan. During the second half of the 20th century, we went too far. We started to define the boundary between our social roles and leisure activities as the boundary between work and life. This was a grave and uncalculated mistake that we are still paying for.

In the 70s and 80s, more and more companies moved toward shareholder supremacy as a management paradigm. Publicly traded companies were dependent on shareholders for investment, and shareholders wanted dividend payouts and increase in share values. And the top-level managers of those companies were no longer the owners themselves. So, when top-level managers wanted to ensure their personal survival, they did so by focusing on shareholders rather than employees.

Organizations no longer existed to make all the Smiths and Taylors more efficient by organizing them into industrial teams. Instead, their skilled labor existed to make more profits for the shareholders in those organizations. One of the new strategies invented for profit-making was to reduce the level of loyalty required by shareholders toward their employees.

In doing so, we dehumanized employees with a new set of terminologies, such as "human resources," or worse, "human capital." While it was difficult for organizational leadership to cull a bunch of their teammates from their economic community, it was easy for them to cut the human resources budget line in favor of stronger year-end net profits. However one framed it; people lost jobs. But in the second scenario, shareholders were one step removed from the human cost of culling. The worker had been placed at the mercy of mere number games. Cutting a portion of employees out from their economic community meant an instant reduction in the cost of operations, which would positively affect the net profit at the end of the year.

To justify this betrayal of employees by consultants and shareholders, social scientists sought to help employees distance themselves from the meaning that humans had found in their labor for generations. They did this by hijacking the language of work-life balance. Employees were told not to bring their work home, and not to let their personal lives interfere with work. This would protect them from taking their business too personally, especially in case of layoffs:

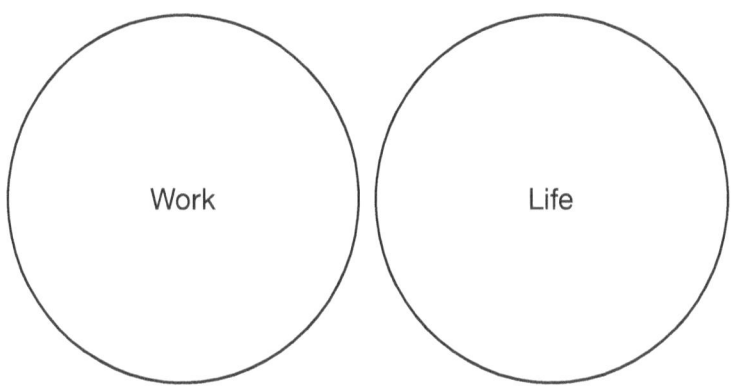

Think about the implications of this brand new language for a minute. Employees weren't members of economic communities as they had been in the early 20th century. They were now called human resources or human capital. And their work was now defined as something "other than" their personal lives. In only 100 years, we devolved from work being your life to work being other than your life. And if work was other than your life, then it didn't really matter if companies cut jobs, because it wasn't impacting your personal life anyway. It was, after all, just a job. You could find another one. The company didn't need to be loyal to its contributing members.

And we bought the lie.

It's not personal. It's just business.

What nonsense! It's not true. It has never been true. And it will never be true. We are what we do. And our work is a huge part of that. Business is personal.

Now, let's go a step further. We are what we do in terms of a job because it's our social role and half of our life. But we also are what we do in terms of our basic behaviors. Hang on, I'll explain.

You Are What You Do

Ahmad (not his real name) was a yeller. I mean loud. I remember sitting in the waiting area outside his office before a meeting and feeling the walls shake. There was a heated conversation going on between what I interpreted to be a terrified employee and his extremely emotional and angry boss. The shouting could be heard throughout the office floor. I imagined the scene inside the office to be a bit like Charlie Brown's parents arguing about whether or not Snoopy is an inside dog. I could picture the exclamation points, curlicues, and shout lines drawn around the office, and that poor employee balled up in a fetal position, spinning involuntary backflips due to the sheer force of wind from Ahmad's voice.

I looked at his assistant and made an awkward teeth-grin emoji face. She responded in kind, adding, "he's often like that." After about 15 minutes, a terrified employee emerged, head down, pale-faced, and quickly shuffled his way down the hall with a vibrating folder of papers in hand. He didn't look anything like Charlie Brown, by the way.

I've known Ahmad for 15 years now, and he has become one of my closest business friends. He was the General Manager of a company that made hundreds of millions of USD in trade every year. And he was one of those managers who sought a balance between love and fear in his employees. You know the type.

Following his outburst, he poked his head out into the waiting area and saw me sitting there. He recalled the volume of his previous conversation, and a veil of embarrassment descended on his face as he invited me in.

"I'm sorry you had to hear that, Dr. Corrie."

"Do you want to talk about it?"

"You know, I don't know why I do that. I don't consider myself the kind of person that yells at his employees like that."

"Well, I have some sad news for you, my friend. Evidence suggests that you are precisely the kind of person that yells at his employees like that."

"Sometimes, it's necessary in order to get the right behavior out of them."

"Is it?"

You see, we humans tend to judge ourselves by our inner intentions. It's a luxury that we afford ourselves that no one else on the planet will ever extend to us. No one is in your head with you. No one can ever know your intentions or your motives. To everyone else on the planet, you are a collection of your words and deeds.

Your intentions are meaningful only to you. To everyone else, you are what you do, regardless of what you intend. I can't even count the number of times I've heard the same dichotomy between deed and intent from my Executive Coaching clients.

I'm not the kind of manager that yells at his employees.

I'm not the kind of mother that hits her kids.

I'm not the kind of CEO that breaks the law.

I'm not the kind of man that cheats on his wife.

I'm not the kind of person that judges people by their skin color.

I'm not the kind of owner that just cuts staff for profit.

I'm not the kind of politician that takes a bribe.

I'm not the kind of consultant that wears checkered Vans with his Zegna suit and Tumi bag.
(Except that I am.)

You get the point. Well, it may be a challenging truth to face, but if you've ever said something like that to try to distance yourself from your behavior, it's a lie. The truth is, you're exactly the kind of person that does what you do. Whatever we do, we were capable of doing both good and bad. Let's look at what that truth means for you.

List three good behaviors that you can identify in yourself:

I'm the kind of person that _____.

I'm the kind of person that _____.

I'm the kind of person that _____.

Now, identify three behaviors of yours that you would like to distance yourself from:

I'm the kind of person that _____.

I'm the kind of person that _____.

I'm the kind of person that _____.

See how cathartic that can be? Just own your behavior. If there are behaviors that you don't like about yourself, you have a choice: you can either change your behavior or change your view of yourself. Ahmad had that choice, too. He could either say:

"I'm the kind of person that yells at his employees;"

or,

"I will stop yelling at my employees."

But what he wasn't allowed to do was to live the lie that he was telling himself.

The good news is that Ahmad calmed down a lot. He learnt to control himself much better, and stopped behaving in a manner that was alienating him from his team.

If you have any behaviors that you would like to expunge from your social identity, it can be done. Just as you are what you do (now), you will be what you will do (in the future).

"I am what I do." Those words and deeds become other peoples' experiences of you. In the same way, you experience other people as a collection of their words and deeds. That's how human lives interact — in an exchange of interpersonal experiences. So, if what you do changes, others' perception of who you are will change too.

Think of human life as a collection of experiences. Our experiences, good and bad, shape our body of knowledge, our worldview, our character, and lead us to behave in a way that we think will be socially and personally effective. And if life is a mosaic of experiences, then how can we not be what we do at, and for, work?

You are Your Job

Remember the lie that we told each other at the end of the 20th century? It's not personal, it's just business? Let's look at that now under this lens of *what we do* being *who we are*.

We spend about a third of our lives sleeping, and our waking life is roughly invested about half of the time in work, and the other half in "not work" activities. Ridiculous consultants and managers would have us believe that the half of our life, during which we are collecting experiences at work, is somehow other than our life. Like this:

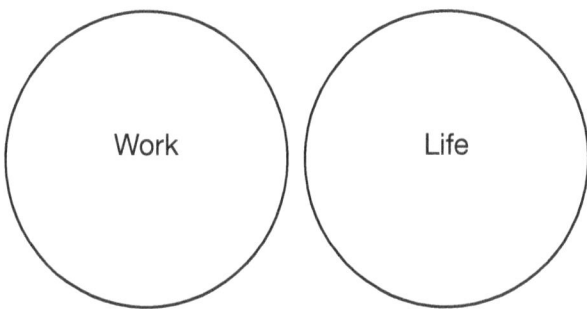

But this isn't true at all. Being at work doesn't mean we're not living our lives. We are alive at work. We are collecting experiences, and those experiences make up half or more of our lives. We are, as people, made up roughly of half work experiences and half not work experiences.

Therefore, you *are* your job.

Your job isn't all of you, but it's definitely not other-than-you. In fact, it's roughly half of you.

And if you are still trying to make the schizophrenic argument that somehow you are two distinct people (work-you and not-work-you), you need to know that not only is that untrue, but it's psychologically unhealthy.

Let's look at it another way. How many social roles do you have?

I'll start by listing some of mine:

Consultant	Father	Student
Professor	Brother	Mentor
Author	Son	Mentee
Husband	Employer	Coach
Friend	Partner	Owner

Let's take two of my social roles associated with the dichotomy above as examples: father and author. Right now, I am writing a book in my author role. Now, the dualists might have you believe that I should punch in and punch out of my work role today, working for eight hours as author, and then stop to resume my role as a father. But that's not how it works with humans. I haven't stopped being a father. Whether I am working as an author, professor, or consultant, I am still 100% a father to my kids. And when I'm with my kids, I'm still 100% author, professor, and consultant.

I am commanding my attention toward my author role at the moment, but I am no less a father while I'm doing that.

Now, it's your turn. I want you to list as many of your social roles as you can.

_____   _____   _____

_____   _____   _____

_____   _____   _____

_____   _____   _____

_____   _____   _____

_____   _____   _____

Does being at work make you less of a parent to your kids (if you have kids)? Of course not. That's ridiculous. Or does being at home with your family make you less of an engineer (if you're an engineer)? Nope.

We are all of our roles, all of the time. That's why we check Facebook at work and check work emails at home. As humans, we fundamentally cannot maintain the dualism between work and life. Because fundamentally, it doesn't exist. It never has. It was an invention of poor management theories in the 70s and 80s.

Let's say, for example, you're at work and your child is rushed to the hospital for an emergency. Do you think your work community will create a way for you to go and be with your child during "work hours"? Of course. I should hope so!

And if you're with your family at a BBQ on a Friday afternoon, and a crisis hits your economic community (your company) and your talents are needed to put out the fire at work, do you think your family will give you leave to address the problem at work on a Friday? It ought to!

There is no such thing as work-life balance. There are no scales called *work* and *life* that need to remain at equilibrium.

There is only work-life blend. You are what you do. It has been true throughout human history, and our brief attempts to divide the two have failed.

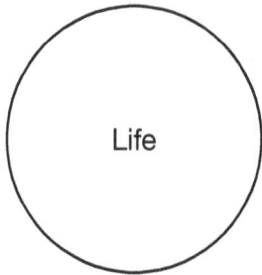

This is your life. Half of it is invested in a work related social role, which contributes to half of your human experience.

So, stop distancing yourself from yourself. Hating your job, psychologically, is a bit like hating half of yourself. It's unhealthy.

Furthermore, it's never just a job. Business is personal.

Mastering your effort and attention to create the best experience for yourself and others in all your social roles is a set of skills. But dividing your identity between work and life is a psychological tragedy. You are what you do (for work).

So be proud of yourself, starting now. Take ownership of your social roles and your good behaviors. If you're an architect, then say it out loud, "I am an architect."

I am an administrative assistant. I am an accountant, flight attendant, web designer, dance instructor, full-time parent, student, delivery driver, plumber, fund manager. Whatever your roles, say them out loud now. Take ownership of them.

And if you are unemployed, don't perceive it as a negative; see it as an opportunity. "I am open to exploring new social roles for myself."

What you're not allowed to do is to say that you are not your job. You are your job. It's not all of you, but it's not other than you either. It's YOUR life, start by owning all of it.

Now you should have some understanding of the meaningfulness of your name, and why people will ask you for your name and your work role within a few questions of meeting you. Those things help people know who you are because, intrinsically, we all know that you are (in part) what you do for work.

It's time to embrace your work-life blend, and the meaningfulness of your name and social role as words that help define you in society. Business is personal, and your business is personal to you.

But if those words, your name and job role, are so meaningful to you and others, then perhaps we need to double click on the meaningfulness of words. Why have these words become so influential in our definition of ourselves? And how can we leverage the power of words to curate higher quality meaning in our lives?

CHAPTER 2

Personal Words are Meaningful

"In the beginning was the Word, and the Word was with God, and the Word was God."

John 1:1

By the time you finish reading this book, you will have a powerful collection of meaningful words designed just for you. It's going to be spectacular!

But first, let's talk about the meaningfulness of words. It's funny when you stop to think about what words actually are, from a physical perspective. They're an imprecise combination of pops, beeps, clicks, hisses, and moans made with our lungs, vocal cords, mouth, and tongue. Have you ever listened to a conversation between two people speaking in a foreign language? It might make you laugh, as it sometimes does to me, when I think of it in these physical terms: two humans throwing clicks and moans at each other to convey some kind of message.

Words can be fun too, so much so that sometimes, we play around with the sound they make and rearrange them to make them sound better.

I slit the sheet, the sheet I slit, and on the slitted sheet, I sit.

He said she sells sea shells by the seashore.

But let's play a little game and see how much meaning can be derived from the smallest combination of words. What if I said …

"I do."

There's a whole story there, right? I don't have to give you any context at all, just three letters properly arranged, and you know that there's a romance going on. It's an event. Lives are changing. It's a wedding.

Let's try another one.

"It's a girl."

I remember those words being said to me. We were in the women's hospital in Tallinn in 2004. My first wife was pregnant with our second child and we were looking at pictures of her on the sonogram for the first time. I remember feeling

Personal Words are Meaningful

overwhelmed by a kind of disharmony of equal parts joy and terror. They were tiny words with massive implications.

What about these sets of words?

"He's gone."

"It's benign."

"You won."

"I love you."

"You idiot."

"Shut up."

"It's over."

"Will you marry me?"

What pictures do these phrases conjure in your mind? In which environments are those kinds of things said? To whom? By who? Do they evoke memories? Places you've been, movies you've seen?

What fascinates me is that although I'm writing this book of over 35,000 words, just a few words can convey a lot of meaning. We humans have packed a lot of meaning into certain words, and in the right combination, even a handful of words can mean something powerful.

Take a minute now and think of a time when someone praised you for something. What did they say? What were the words that you remember that made a difference to you?

_____

_____

And can you remember a time when someone said something that hurt you? What were those meaningful words?

_____

_____

What's in a Name?

The words we use to describe ourselves are very important as well. Let's start with the first word that was assigned to describe us – our first name.

As I mentioned in Chapter 1, your first name is likely destined to become your favorite word, but did you know that it also has an impact on the kind of person you might become? It's that powerful! In fact, the study of the influence of first names on life and career choices is called *nominative determinism*. There's a whole science surrounding it. Psychologically, it's probably not because your name has any intrinsic or objective value, but rather because people tend to make subconscious decisions that align their life to their idea of what their name means. It's the reason why there is a significantly higher proportion of dentists named Dennis than there are dentists with equally common names such as Larry or Walter.[4]

The term nominative determinism was first introduced in the November 5, 1994 edition of *New Scientist*, which highlighted the following examples of the phenomenon:

> We recently came across a new book, *Pole Positions — The Polar Regions and the Future of the Planet*, by Daniel Snowman. Then, a couple of weeks later, we received a copy of *London Under London — A Subterranean Guide*, one of the authors of which is Richard Trench. So, it was interesting to see Jen Hunt of the University of Manchester stating in the October issue of *The Psychologist*: "Authors gravitate to the area of research which fits their surname." Hunt's example is an article on incontinence in the *British Journal of Urology* by A. J. Splatt and D. Weedon.[5]

---

[4] Robb, A., *If Your Name Is Dennis, You're More Likely to Become a Dentist*. Retrieved December 1, 2019, from https://newrepublic.com/article/116140/psychologists-say-our-names-affect-what-careers-we-choose

[5] Feedback. (1994). New Scientist, *(November 5)*.

Honestly, an article on incontinence by Splatt and Weed on? You can't make this stuff up. My name is Corrie. Yes, like Corrie Ten Boom, the famous Nazi Holocaust escapee. My parents chose the feminine spelling of my name, and perhaps that's one of the influences behind why I ended up in the social sciences, studying history, religion, psychology, and leadership.

I have an awkward collection of memories stemming from my name, one of which is that my mother used to dress me up like a girl when I was a child. I had blonde curly hair until I was about five, and my mother liked to get to me to wear a dress for a couple of hours and collect compliments about what a beautiful girl she had. I don't remember those occasions (selective memory, perhaps?), but I've seen the photos and that was traumatic enough.

I did dress in drag for Halloween when I was 14 years old. We were living in Ottawa, and I had a dress, wig, makeup, the whole thing. I was a skinny kid and with tennis balls stuffed in my bra, I looked so much like a girl that often, when I knocked on peoples' doors to say "trick or treat," they would respond with curiosity about what my costume was supposed to be. They thought I was a girl too lazy to wear a costume. I looked a bit like Tootsie, so I don't know if I had won or lost the game when I corrected them in my newly descended male voice. Now-a-days, I expect they would have laughed less and apologized more, and offered more candy in exchange for my forgiveness for them having assumed my gender.

But it was Halloween, I was a kid, and I had set myself up for those awkward moments.

It wasn't long after that that I received samples in the mail from a feminine hygiene company. They had, undoubtedly, gender-biased my name from a spreadsheet somewhere thinking I would be in the market for tampons sometime around my 16th birthday. I wasn't. But they do come in handy when you sustain a wound while roughing it in the wild. Sterile cotton makes for a good dressing.

Throughout my life, I've been assumed female by nearly everyone who's read my name and not seen my picture or heard my voice. There's even a second Dr. Corrie Block out there on the internet, believe it or not. You guessed it. Female.

I don't have any lingering sexual hang-ups stemming from my name. Although I sometimes wonder if I may be more empathic, more in touch with my feminine side, more of a champion of gender inclusion in the workplace because of it. I'm certainly convinced that it has influenced who I am and what I'm doing with my life.

My last name is Block, a very masculine, strong name. So perhaps, the two balance each other out. Then again, perhaps, I wrote my previous book, *Spartan CEO*, in some small subconscious part, to defend my masculinity. I'll leave it to the Freuds of the world to ponder on that one.

How might the name Block have influenced me? In the sense that "blockhead" is a moniker for an idiot, perhaps I rebelled by collecting post-graduate degrees to exhibit my intellect. But I find the influence of my name a bit more visible in the sense that Block indicates a defensive or contrarian position. Throughout my career, I have actively defended truths – religious, historical, philosophical, and organizational. I have leant toward a maverick stance, defining and defending, alone if necessary, sacred spaces, sacred texts, sacred humanitarian concerns, and sacred ideas about the value of human lives.

The Names We Call Ourselves

It follows from the previous discussion that when we look at the meaningfulness of words, we would do well to start with those by which we refer to ourselves. Think of your first, middle, and last names, and what they mean, and how they sound as words.

In what ways do you exhibit behaviors in your life that reflect your given name?

_____

_____

Arguably, our given names (or nicknames) were among the first meaningful personalized words we heard, since they were the first words we recognized as having specific reference to us as individual humans, separate from our parents, and separate from other humans. But they are not the only names we call ourselves. We may describe ourselves with other monikers and adjectives, often critical and unflattering. We may look in the mirror and call ourselves …

Stupid

Ugly

Fat

Useless

Weak

… or any number of other words that we create as revealing descriptors of ourselves. Now, if your given name can have a long-term subconscious and psychological effect on your life decisions, how much more influence might the words you use to describe yourself be wielding? How powerful is your criticism of yourself? And what subconscious influences do the underlying narratives have on your decision-making, your conduct?

Let's take an inventory of those meaningful words for a second. When you are alone, what words do you use to criticize yourself?

_____ _____ _____

_____   _____   _____

_____   _____   _____

Don't worry, we'll deal with these in a minute. For now, I just want you to get them out on paper so they're not running amok in your head. Writing things down is a powerful step.

Do you want to know what my words were? Fat, Weak, Failure, and Incompetent. Those were my internal narratives. No one saw them but me, and they kept me from pursuing my best life.

As it turns out, there's a direct relationship between self-criticism and goal pursuit. Not shocking, but a number of studies show that your self-criticism will hinder your efforts to pursue and achieve your goals.[6] We'll work on your personal goals in Chapter 7. But let's, for now, just acknowledge the meaningfulness of the words we tell ourselves.

If we tell ourselves that we are fat, ugly, and stupid, then science shows that we will make decisions that lead us in the direction of fulfilling those descriptions as prophecies. The most sickening part of this downward spiral is that not only will we make decisions that may manifest the very adjectives we use to describe ourselves; we actually give ourselves

---

6 Mossholder, K. W., Richardson, H. A., & Settoon, R. P. (2011). *Human Resource Systems and Helping in Organizations: A Relational Perspective.* Academy of Management Review, 36*(1), 33-52.*

credit for having justified that adjective the closer we get to fulfilling it. For example, the fatter you get, the more you will reward yourself for being right about having described yourself as being fat in the first place. That cycle will keep you from making decisions that can lead you out of the cycle of your being (or feeling) fat.

Humans are weird. But hackable.

If words are so meaningful that they subconsciously influence our decision-making in a way that fulfills our ideas of those words, does it follow that we can hack ourselves by choosing different words?

You bet we can!

Now, I want you to revisit those critical words you used to describe yourself above, and choose positively framed words to replace them.

For example, "stupid" might be reframed as "unique," since no one has your particular blend of knowledge and experience.

Ugly	Distinctive
Fat	Cuddly
Useless	Chilled Out
Weak	Agile

Now, I want you to try it with your words here:

_____   _____   _____

_____   _____   _____

_____   _____   _____

Great! Now look in a mirror and describe yourself with these new words. I know it seems a bit forced, but trust me, the more often you do it, the better. You'll make different kinds of decisions once you start believing the words you choose to describe yourself. You will end up becoming what you describe. We can't help it. We're human after all.

If words that we tell ourselves can have that kind of influence on us, what influence can the words of others have?

What do you think?

The Meaningful Words of Others

It's the same. If a boss calls his employees idiots, they will tend toward idiocy. If a mother calls her son the devil's child, he might very well become one. And if a group of teens call their classmate a loser, guess what? Yes, they start to tell themselves that same narrative, and it leads to poorer quality decision-making due to lower self-esteem.

Take a look at those critical words you used to describe yourself. How many of them originated with you, and how many of them are based on things other people said to you, or other peoples' expectations of you? Nearly all of them will have originated from outside of you.

Our tendency is to be generous with ourselves unless we receive feedback from someone outside of us that we respect. It might be a parent, a teacher, a friend, an enemy, a boss, a magazine, a TV show, or a celebrity influencer on Instagram. We're social creatures, so we tend to value the voices of our society when we think they are talking about us. Fact is, your internal view of yourself is pretty strong, until you allow others to change it for you. And if it can change once, it can change again.

I recall having walked off stage after a keynote speech at a major event feeling really good about myself. I had worked on my presentation and put in practice to make it powerful and engaging. I had hit my mark, and the audiences' response was tremendous. Then an executive in attendance approached me to have a short conversation about leadership during which she told me, "You're a much better speaker than Simon Sinek."

Now, it has never been important for me to compete with Simon, and there is no way of objectively substantiating this woman's claim, but it doesn't matter ... because whether better or not, I saw myself in Simon's league as a public speaker for the first time that day. And her words changed my view of myself.

Now, let's look at your job again. What are your narratives for the half of your life that you are investing in your social role at work? Go ahead and put a checkmark beside the statements that feel true for you in the list below.

I love my job.	I hate my job.
I'm good at my job.	I suck at my job.
The people I work with like me.	The people I work with don't like me.
I like the people I work with.	I don't like the people I work with.
My job is fun.	My job sucks.
I have a clear career path ahead of me.	I don't know what my next step is.
I feel engaged at work.	I feel disengaged at work.
My company has good products/services.	My company has bad products/services.
I like my boss.	I dislike my boss.

I like my CEO.   I dislike my CEO.

Now, take a look at the list. Are your checkmarks mostly on the right side or left side? What kind of influence might these narratives be having on your experience of work? Remember, it's not just a job, it's half of your life. So, if your experience of work is a predominantly negative one, then half of your life (at least) is filled with negative experiences. If your experience at work is predominantly positive, then half of your life (and probably much more) is made up of positive experiences.

I now want you to look back at your answers to the two questions that I asked Ben when we first met.

"Are you good at your job?"

"Do you enjoy it?"

Your answers to these questions are influencing your experience at work. If you said anything less than a yes to both of these questions, then you're contributing to your own lack of satisfaction at work. You are less engaged than you could be, and half of your life is less meaningful than it really should be.

It's time to take ownership of your life, especially the half of it that you've invested in your current economic community. You have options. You can change your job, or you can change the way you experience your job. Either way, you're going to need a strategic plan. And that's where we're going now. We're taking the meaningfulness of work and the meaningfulness of words, and we're going to combine them in the most core set of words at work: your corporate strategy.

CHAPTER 3

Corporate Words are Meaningful

Organizational Words

In the social sciences, we've discovered that humans have difficulty organizing themselves in groups of more than 150 without the creation of some kind of objective text. Humans in large groups need meaningful words. Sometimes they are constitutions, contracts, sacred texts, mantras, MOUs, policy manuals, employee handbooks, epic poems, organizational charts, or sets of laws.

The earliest surviving texts vary in content. They range from the Egyptian pyramid instructions for how to properly bury a Pharaoh, to the Epic of Gilgamesh — perhaps the first great work of fiction, to the Indian Rigveda, which contains chants and hymns for worship.

Back before text was text, humans in large groups arranged themselves according to sacred words from sacred leaders. Human representatives of the divine, declared on behalf of their gods how humans should be organized and by which rules they should live. The first five books of Moses (Torah) from the Bible are foundational scriptures for all Christians,

Muslims, and Jews, governing about half of the human population at that time. It is a collection of histories, stories, poetry, census data, and laws by which the early Jews were organized. The Torah mentions a text that even predates itself: the 10 commandments, inscribed in stone, outlined the top 10 rules for life, as prescribed for the Jewish nation.

In its early years, the Torah was passed down orally, not as text. Having the 10 commandments appear in the story as written texts, however, indicates to historians that a written Hebrew language already existed at the time when the story was first told. And so, older texts, than the oldest we have discovered, must also have existed.

So roughly speaking, for the last 12,000 to 15,000 years, we have been using meaningful words to organize ourselves. These meaningful words need not be texts; their meaning may be expressed in speech or in song:

> I have a dream.

> One small step for man, one giant leap for mankind.

> All we need is love.

> This is the song that never ends,
> it just goes on and on, my friends ...

My point is that humans bond in groups over collections of words that their groups find meaningful. We've been doing it since the beginning of recorded history, and likely for centuries before that. We not only need meaningful words to keep groups of humans organized, we also can't get very far without them.

Here are a few examples:

> All human beings are born free and equal in dignity and rights. They are endowed with reason and conscience and should act towards one another in a spirit of brotherhood.[7]
>
> From Article 1 of the UN Universal Declaration of Human Rights.

> We the People of the United States, in Order to form a more perfect Union, establish Justice, insure domestic Tranquility, provide for the common defence, promote the general Welfare, and secure the Blessings of Liberty to ourselves and our Posterity, do ordain and establish this Constitution for the United States of America.[8]
>
> From the preamble to the Constitution of the USA.

---

[7] *Universal Declaration of Human Rights. (1948). Retrieved December 10, 2019, from https://www.un.org/en/universal-declaration-human-rights/.*
[8] *Constitution of the United States (1776).*

> In the name of Allah, the most gracious, the most merciful. Praise be to Allah, the lord of the universe. The most gracious, the most merciful. Master of the Day of Judgment. You alone we worship, and you alone we ask for help. Guide us to the straight path. The path of those on whom you have bestowed your grace, not of those who earned wrath, nor of those who have gone astray.[9]
>
> The opening surah of the Qur'an.

> Our mission is to organize the world's information and make it universally accessible and useful.[10]
>
> The vision and mission statement of Google.

> Rowing is and always will be our reason for being. Sydney Rowing Club's goal is to be Australia's best rowing club achieved through the pursuit of excellence, performance at the highest standards and the development of strength and quality of character within our members. We wish to build and support high quality programs and facilities that promote access to and excellence in rowing and use rowing as

---

9 Holy Qur'an
10 About Google. Retrieved December 12, 2019, from about.google

a means to foster physical activity, health, leadership, and community engagement.[11]

> From the Sydney Rowing Club
> Member's Handbook

Whether it's knowing who is included in the definition of humanity, or clarifying in which direction humans who call themselves Muslims should pray; whether divinely inspired or as guidance for how to connect with other people who love rowing, humans need meaningful words. We love them. They bring us together and help us to align small and large pieces of our lives. Like vows at a wedding ceremony, all kinds of words provide the glue that holds our social roles together and gives us shared expectation on identity, inclusion, responsibilities, authorities, and boundaries.

Family Words

Even families have meaningful words that get repeated until they become part of the oral history of the family. I asked my kids recently for some of the meaningful words by which our family is organized: something that we Blocks often say that

---

11 *Sydney Rowing Club Handbook. (2019). Retrieved December 15, 2019, from https://www.sydneyrowingclub.com.au/wp-content/uploads/2019/11/Sydney-Rowing-Club-Handbook-Rev-4.5-22-October-2019.pdf*

helps us in life. They both produced mantras of mine that I've been using since they were tiny, to prepare them for adulthood.

Son (20): It's better to have it and not need it, than to need it and not have it.

Daughter (16): What do we do when we fall down? Get up and try again.

One of my first wife's mantras that I still live by is this: We're not raising kids, we're raising adults.

Here's one of my daughter's mantras: Good job for good job.

My daughter first said this when she was learning to understand sarcasm. She had made something and showed it to her older brother for feedback, who replied, "good job!" It was his habit at the time to use the term, "good job!" sarcastically, sometimes accompanied by a sinister smile and a forced thumbs-up to clarify that the meaning of the words was in fact opposite to their commonly accepted interpretation. "Good job," could mean everything from "I'm proud of you," to, "no one cares," which is a difficult range of meaning to be deciphered, especially for a young girl. So, she asked him for clarification, "Good job for good job? Or good job for bad job?"

We had a good laugh about that and the mantra has cemented itself in our family for more than a decade now.

We've been saying it to each other ever since. It's so much part of the fabric of our family that at my wedding to my second wife, when my son was invited to say something at the ceremony, he included it: "good job for good job." It was a Blockism to ensure there was no sarcasm or ambiguity in his congratulations on our wedding. It was meaningful to us in a way that it could have only been meaningful to us. It was our shared language.

These Blockisms are carefully worded to sound like they might have been quoted from a "rules of life" document. They are a part of the Block family corpus of meaningful words. If we had a Block family constitution, these would be articles. Yet, this is probably the first time I've written them down anywhere. And they aren't likely unique to my family; if you've heard them elsewhere, I wouldn't be surprised.

What are some of the meaningful words that you carry from your family? Do you remember sayings from your parents or siblings that became meaningful words by which your family lived? Write one or two of them down here:

_____

_____

Using meaningful words to communicate worldviews has been a practice of mine throughout my entire career. I learned it informally from one of my mentors, Kory Sorensen, when I was a teenager. He was a pastor in my church, and he had a mantra that has stayed with me for the last 30 years:

"The most important thing in your life is your relationship with God. Apart from that, everything else is irrelevant." – Kory Sorensen.

It's perhaps a bit on the extreme side, a bit like when Jesus said: "If you want to be my disciple, you must, by comparison, hate everyone else — your father and mother, wife and children, brothers and sisters — yes, even your own life. Otherwise, you cannot be my disciple." Luke 14:6 (NLT).

Taken out of context, these words can be misunderstood as promoting hatred of family, but they're really not. Anyone that knows the teachings of Jesus, or Kory, knows that their intent is to draw hyperbolic contrast between the love of God and the love of family, with the former being the more important of the two loves.

In my work as an author, speaker, and strategist, I have a small collection of meaningful words that my clients and co-workers have heard me say with some regularity. Here are a few of them:

- Words are meaningful.
- Meetings are the most expensive hours in a company's day.

Corporate Words are Meaningful

- There is no "company," only a corporate community.
- It's not a job, it's half your life.
- Every decision you've ever made has led you here.
- Time spent is not a measure of productivity.
- We are what we do.
- Business is personal.
- Transparency builds trust, and trust builds transparency.
- Authority + Accountability = Empowerment.
- Motivation gets you to the starting line, discipline gets you to the finish line.
- Personal vision + Corporate vision = Meaningful Management.
- Strategy without a story is just work; and a story without strategy is just rhetoric.
- Regret is to the past what worry is to the future. But worry is worse, because it's like regretting something that hasn't even happened.
- If you aim for nothing, you will certainly achieve it.
- Pull the trigger, nudge the bullet.

This next one was repeated back to me by my daughter when I told her I was thinking about proposing to my second wife.

For context, my first wife and I had been married for 22 years. It was an intense relationship filled with amazing adventures, and I'm so grateful for all of the wonderful memories and our two brilliant children. Eventually, my ex-wife decided to go on an adventure that I couldn't join her for, and so the marriage ended amicably.

Eighteen months later, my daughter and my soon-to-be fiancé had developed a good relationship. I asked her what she thought about me proposing to Nicole, and she was thrilled. She wanted to know if I was planning to propose the following week. I was a bit shocked. It was too soon. I wasn't prepared for her overwhelmingly supportive response, and I didn't have a ring yet, so she handed my words back to me.

She said:

"When you know what you want to do with your life, you want your life to start as soon as possible."

These axioms are instances where my meaningful words bridge my work-life blend, and show where my character influences the advice I give to my clients and colleagues. They are an informal policy that I bring to the table. Do you have sets of words like that? What are some of the things you say often in order to encourage the people around you to align themselves to your values? Write one or two of them here:

_____

_____

_____

We all have them: meaningful words. We've been using them as a best practice for building and maintaining relationships and clarifying expectations for the whole of human history. We still use them every day, though we're often not aware of it. Even rarer still are the times we design and deploy them intentionally to their full effect. One of the places where they are often created and rarely fully utilized is in the corporate world – the world of half your life, the world where most of your time is invested with other humans on an economic project that keeps your family fed, your kids educated, your parents cared for, and makes your dreams true.

Economic Community Words

> "Sometimes it's nation against nation, or tribe against tribe. Sometimes it's neighbor against neighbor. But today, it's just me against my brother, praise God."
>
> — Old Yemeni proverb

I don't like using the terms corporation or company. I use them because they're clear in meaning, but I find that they are too cold to describe the economic communities that humans have designed to compete peacefully with each other for the planet's finite resources. We used to compete with each other in military contests, literally killing each other over land and resources. We humans have a violent history.

Ancient humans were horrible to each other.[12] But we're slowly emerging from gathering resources through murder, slavery, and theft into a more civilized game that began with the ubiquity of trade. Since the Industrial Revolution, we've been on an escalating path toward competing with each other through teams of humans organized around economic projects, like selling car tires, making things from oil, or crafting new restaurant dishes. Our shift from military to economic competition has led to a paradox: while there are more humans alive to compete than ever before, fewer and fewer of us are raping and pillaging our way to success. That's good, right? We should celebrate that more.

We're still human, after all. This shift to economic competition meant that we needed new kinds of meaningful words to live by. We have strategy documents now, organization charts, and employee handbooks. These texts help us organize ourselves, so we know how we should play our part in a larger team of humans to compete with other teams in elaborate economic games.

I was 25 years old when I began consulting with economic communities to draft their meaningful words. I started with a standard strategy statement comprised of vision, mission, values, and goals. It was a lot of fun.

---

12 Pinker, S. (2011). The Better Angels of Our Nature: Why Violence Has Declined. *New York: Viking.*

I'd get the organization's leaders into a room for a couple of days, and we would debate the direction of the community, it's collective character, and the economic arenas in which it would compete.

But after a decade of doing this, I noticed something that really irritated me.

No one read them.

These meaningful words that we sweated and debated over would end up as plaques on the boardroom wall, or as content for the About Us page on the company website. But not only did the members of the team not know them, the leaders who produced them often couldn't recall them just a few months later. All of the excitement and effort of putting them together was lost.

Can you recall the vision statement of any of the economic communities in which you have worked?

Now pick one. Choose one community that, at some point, you had been dedicating half of your human experience to, and look up its vision or mission statement online. Hint: It's probably on the About Us page of their website. Write it here:

_____

_____

Imagine that at some point, the leaders of the organization sat in a room together, hotly debating these words, choosing them, defining them, and taking care to convey as much intent as possible through them. Do the words mean more to you now?

The Emirates Macaroni Factory is the oldest manufacturing company in Dubai. They've been making pasta for 40 years. When their founder passed away several years ago, his eldest son took the reins, and with a few hundred employees, he felt the weight of responsibility for the community that his father had built and left to him as a legacy. I was invited to lead the restructuring effort, and as a part of it, I encouraged Ahmed (a different Ahmed to the yeller I told you about earlier) to produce a new set of meaningful words for the community.

We spent four days in a hotel conference room along with the six key leaders in the company, including the newly hired General Manager and HR Manager. We brainstormed on the key areas that we wanted to define as part of the legacy. We debated some and easily agreed on others.

What struck me about this particular organization was that the rookies in the room were just as passionately contributing to the conversation as were the veterans with 20+ years of experience. Whether an employee or an owner, each felt valued in the community, and each knew they were dedicating a significant portion of their lives to the pasta game. What kind of team would they be? What kind of game would they play? What was the output of this wonderful, clarifying conversation?

vision
We are a leading regional
FMCG company.

mission
A legacy of satisfied consumers,
employees, and other stakeholders,
empowered by our portfolio of quality,
innovative, and healthy products.

values
Quality, Authenticity, Solidarity,
Excellence, Heritage

goals
Customers, Shareholders, Employees,
Distributors, Community

I can't share their strategic goals with you because that would be a breach of my Non-Disclosure Agreement with them, but I can share the five areas above in which they defined measurable results for achieving their vision.

I remember the last day vividly, when I had all of these things up on a single slide for them to see for the first time. The walls were covered in used flipchart paper, with words circled and scratched out, sentences in multiple revisions, and lists of ideas both accepted and discarded by the team.

I addressed the new General Manager, and gesturing to the strategy slide on the wall, I asked him, "Is this the kind of community that you want to dedicate half of your life to each day?" He was thrilled. It was a strong "yes." But I didn't stop there. Addressing each of the members of the team, I asked them the same question, each time eliciting the same response. Until I got to Ahmed. There, across the boardroom table in the hotel, and having heard the dedication of his team to his father's legacy, I asked him, "Ahmed, is this your father's company?"

And with tears in his eyes, he replied,

"Yes, this is our company."

The words were meaningful enough to bond the team emotionally, transparently, and with a declaration of individual dedication to the meaningfulness of feeding families, educating kids, and caring for parents through the manufacture and distribution of pasta. The words would not be so easily forgotten this time.

If you're working for a company right now, I want you to look up your company's vision, mission, and values statement. It might be called a Why statement, or a Purpose statement. That doesn't matter, just see if you can find any meaningful words written by the leaders of your organization and write them out here. You'll refer to them again later. If you aren't working at the moment, or your company doesn't have these statements written down, then use a company you like as a sample set.

vision: _____

_____

mission: _____

_____

values: _____

_____

We write these strategy statements through the heat of debate and with the passion of poets because we are human, and deep down, we know that we've always needed them. But often, we forget to use them. Perhaps this is because our modern games are economic ones, without the urgency of life or death. And perhaps, because we've become too passive about the psychological needs of humans to be aligned, motivated, and encouraged by the mantras, mottos, and axioms that come from shared sets of meaningful words.

So, I changed my practice.

A few years ago, I decided that I wasn't going to help an economic community clarify its strategy unless those who were involved in the process did so for themselves at the same time. So, as we produced a vision, mission, and set of values for the organization, we simultaneously did the same for every participant in the discussion. This had tangible benefits.

First, the leaders at the table could see their own personal strategies overlapping with those of the organization. This was a good thing, since they too had dedicated half of their human experience to the project.

Second, participants could learn about each other in a more transparent and interpersonal way. They could see from each other's personal strategies why each of them had chosen to dedicate half of their lives to this particular economic project for a while. This built transparency, and transparency, built trust.

Third, having seen that the economic community's words were based on their own, they could also see how it was a collective of human aspirations rather than one centralized project. Every corporate community is the composition of the personal visions and goals of its members.

These words can, if properly formed and communicated, live in the hearts of those who have dedicated half of their lives to executing the projects that they represent. But to properly value these community statements, we should start with ourselves.

Your Personal Words

I was in my twenties when I first wrote down my vision, mission, values, and goals. It's been a living document of mine ever since. It is the meaningful words I arrange my life around. It governs my decisions and helps me plan where to invest my resources of time, effort, and finances. It is an anchor for me, a kind of curated individual constitution that gives me guidance, especially during turbulent times. I tweak it, every year at least, and sometimes during major events in my life, one of which I'll tell you about in the next chapter.

For the remainder of this book, you will be building your personal life strategy. This is a process through which I've led, literally, thousands of executive coaching clients and corporate managers. Doing so has helped many of my former clients make significant life decisions, and find more meaningful lives in the process.

It's a well-known fact now that people who describe their lives as meaningful live longer, are healthier, and happier. But there are a few things you will need to keep in mind if we're going to do this together.

Happiness is Not the Goal

All humans experience happiness in essentially the same way from a neurological perspective – as a combination of dopamine, oxytocin, and serotonin, sometimes with endorphins or anandamide mixed in. These chemicals are produced and consumed primarily in our brains. Though different humans have different triggers for the production of happiness chemicals, all human happiness is composed of this particular cocktail.

The good news is that happiness can be obtained in a number of different ways. For example, getting likes on Facebook, eating a Big Mac, exercise, taking drugs, avoiding a risk, drinking alcohol, hugging your mother, handing in a report, or watching TV. The bad news is that although most of these activities lead to happiness from a neurochemical standpoint, the neurochemistry of happiness is very short-lived. It goes away pretty quickly, and then, happiness junkies end up looking for the next high of happiness.

I like Moustafa Hamwi's comments on this point. In his book, *Live Passionately*, Hamwi titles one of his chapters, *The Pursuit of Happiness is Making You Sad*.[13] And I think he's right. Happiness is a good thing but not the best thing. If not strategically managed, then it can end up being a short-term distraction from long-term fulfillment. Fulfillment is the satisfaction of doing the right things with the required amount of effort to achieve something truly meaningful. And it's very different from happiness.

---

13 Hamwi, M. (2019). Live Passionately: The Blueprint to Design a Life Truly Worth Living. *Melbourne, VC, Australia: Passionpreneur Publishing.*

I can tell you now that a number of the most meaningful things I've achieved in my life have been only sparsely sprinkled with happiness along the way. Running 45 kms of obstacle course races in two days was very fulfilling, but with bloodied feet and injured muscles, I didn't spend much of that time in a state of happiness.

I wrote the majority of my masters and doctoral degrees alone, when I was tired, under pressure, working full-time, and all I wanted to do was sleep. Though they were all very fulfilling in terms of information and accomplishment, I spent much of that time in a very unhappy state.

Of the 10,000 hours that Malcolm Gladwell says it takes to become an expert in something, how many hours do you think are spent in a state of happiness?[14] And how much of it is just mind-numbing practice, discipline, and getting up when you feel like staying down? In truth, most worthwhile things are not a matter of happiness, they're a matter of fulfillment, and fulfillment requires discipline.

Be of Sober Mind

You should be reading this book and doing the exercises at a time of day when you are free of distractions and can put some concentrated effort into them. Don't do this when

---

14 Gladwell, M. (2011). Outliers: The Story of Success. *New York: Back Bay Books.*

you're distracted, or exhausted. You'll be designing your life, so give it proper focus.

I think best in the morning. I wake up most days at 5 am, I'm in the gym by 6 am, and at my computer by 7:30 am. From then, I have a good 4-5 hours of uninterrupted time to concentrate on my clients' core challenges. I give the hardest things my best time. Try to carve out time for the following four chapters during your best time.

It's Not Set in Stone

Whatever you write can be changed. There's no one judging you and there are no wrong answers. You'll be writing about yourself, and whatever you write is completely subjective. So have fun with it, and write in pencil if you can, so you can edit as you go along.

I think my personal vision, mission, values, and goals have gone through more than a hundred iterations. Over time, my vision solidified first. I edited it less and less over the years. My mission changed when my kids were born, when I changed countries, started my post-graduate education, published my books, got divorced, and got married again.

My first list of values had 11 words on it, which I'll share with you in Chapter 6. It stayed like that for a few years. Then I started to review it more often. I realized in my 30s that some words were absorbed by others. Some were me wishing they were values and recognizing that they actually weren't values at all, but ideals. And some words were added to reflect my actual behaviors more accurately, not just my intentions.

Whatever you write, you can change. I typically review my meaningful words at least once every year, if only to set new annual goals for myself, some of which I'll share with you later on in this book.

Transparency Builds Trust, and Trust Builds Transparency

When I have done this personal strategy work with teams of executives, it is always with the willingness to set the example on transparency. At the end of this book, I hope you will be willing to share your vision, mission, values, and goals with me. In the spirit of reciprocity, I will lead by sharing mine with you. As we go through this journey together, you will get to read my vision, mission, values, and goals. I practice what I preach.

I already feel a bit more exposed just having written that. It's one thing to share my vision with an executive coaching client, but I feel more exposed when I share it with a board of directors, and even more so when I share it with a workshop full of executives. But this is my first time writing it down for publication to the whole world. I feel a bit naked, to be honest. Not that I want you to think of me naked (don't make it weird). I'm just saying that even with 20 years of experience,

30,000 hours of education, and having shared this with thousands of leaders, I'm still feeling a bit vulnerable. I hope the risk is worth it. I hope it builds the trust with you that I am hoping for.

Now that we've got that out of the way, let's begin, shall we?

CHAPTER 4

Mutual Vision: Why you're in your role

My Vision

It's a beautiful Sunday morning to go to church in Vancouver, Canada. A man in his 60s strolls up to the front of the crowd, and placing his hand on the simple urn on the table at the front of the room, he raises his gaze, smiles, and begins to speak.

> My father was not a perfect man, but he was an honorable man, and in spite of his recent death, I am confident that he is also immortal, as he always claimed to be. He lived a passionate life on a series of adventures that he carved out for himself. Together with his first wife, Dawn, he raised his kids in Estonia just after the fall of the Soviet Union, and then in Yemen, just prior to and during the war in early 2010. From there, he moved to Dubai, where his life and career began to grow in prominence.
>
> He never quite fit into the church environment in which he was raised, and in spite of dedicating two decades

to the institution, he struggled to find an adequate expression of his faith within its walls. His arms were too wide, his mind too open. Yet his relationship with God was a private affair for him, deeply rooted in his sense of calling, but somehow always creeping out through his hands and feet, through his ongoing charity work in Yemen, and his heart for humanity which is woven like a golden thread through his eclectic volume of written works.

He loved very deeply. His children — both those born to him, and those gifted to him through his second marriage — would, if they could all stand with me today, echo the same. He held no concern for what we did in terms of a career path, but instead concentrated his efforts and input on who we would become as people. He was proud of us, not because of what we accomplished, but because of who we were. All five of us, too, are very proud to have been under his care, and we have each learned to care for others through his example.

His second wife, Nicole, often remarked that my father would go out of his way to find small, nearly hidden ways to improve the quality of her life on a daily basis. As he has done with many of you here today. He was effortlessly selfless in the practicality of his love for those close to him. Through her stories, I learned who he was in secret, a generous and loyal friend.

He was curious about the world. Always in pursuit of a more interesting question, and always keen to risk himself in the quest for raising the bar on what could be done in a single human life. It was a rare thing to have a conversation with my father about sports, the weather, or the news, that did not somehow quickly evolve into a discussion about the human condition, the meaning of life, or some word of wisdom that he would insert into our heads like slivers of challenging encouragement. He influenced us to always strive to be the best versions of ourselves, and so we did.

He was not a rich man, in part because he often chose the road less travelled, and in part because he was generous, a trait he had learned from his father, and his father's father before him. But money was a means for him, never a goal. He did not cling to any worldly thing as much as he did to relationships, ideas, experiences, meaningful words, and the curation of his legacy in a corpus of texts on topics ranging from Islamic history, peacemaking, executive performance, and product design, to collections of poetry, fiction, and some of the best organizational leadership works of his day.

Having left his voice echoing through a dozen academic disciplines, and in the minds of tens of thousands of grateful followers, he has indeed curated his own immortality. I believe him now. He will live forever, in the halls of some of the world's highest performing organizations, in the hearts of the world's most empathic leaders, and lie in wait in his eternal texts to satisfy the curiosity of yet unborn leaders who will read his works for centuries to come. And perhaps, above all of this, he may yet be alive in the heaven that he believed in, where he has finally achieved the only approval that he ever really craved, that of his God, the quiet craftsman of his personal destiny.

Corrie Jonn Block was indeed an honorable father and husband, a polymath scholar, and a globally recognized business strategist. And as he often did throughout his 20s, I would like to raise a tribute in his own words. Please join me in a toast: "To life, and death, and life again." I miss you, dad. You are a good man.

And with that, my funeral will end, and the earth will go on hurtling itself around the sun, without me on it this time. And if I can get anything close to that said of me at the celebration of my life, then I know I will have done what I was placed on this earth to do. I will have lived the dream, left my legacy, accomplished my vision, and can now, rest in peace.

Now, take a brief look at my LinkedIn profile. Honestly, connect with me there and look through my profile for a minute. Trust me, there's a point to this.

www.linkedin.com/in/corrieblock

And have a quick browse through my website, for fun.

www.drcorrieblock.com

Ok, did you notice anything in my profile?

How much of my eulogy from above was evident in my public profile?

What are the things that are most meaningful to me that you can see online?

Did I mention my professional positions or my academic degrees in my eulogy?

My certifications, famous connections, number of likes and followers on social media? Were any of these mentioned?

No, because those things aren't my vision, they're just yardsticks and milestones along the way. My vision is higher than that, more personal, more ambitious. Here it is in its exact wording on the day of this writing:

vision
To be an honorable father and husband, a polymath scholar, and a globally recognized business strategist.

That's my vision.

What is a Vision Statement?

Ok, now this part is going to get some interesting responses from the audience, I think. I've been in strategy for two decades now, and I've read every kind of definition there is.

Simon Sinek, one of the best leadership speakers of the last decade, calls it your "Why." He says that it should be simple, clear, actionable, in affirmative language, and focused on how you will bring value to others.[15] I like this definition because it's elegant. But then, he says that it should be in a single sentence, and I find that a bit restrictive for some people and some companies. I've seen great statements both for individuals and corporations that are written as sentences, a couple of sentences, a collection of phrases, and sometimes, just as one or two words, such as Apple's corporate vision statement, "We Believe."

Bestselling authors Hector Garcia and Francesc Miralles develop a Japanese approach to vision called *Ikigai*, meaning "reason for being."[16] They describe an old concept of life purpose in a blend of four arenas of human activity: what we love, what we're good at, what we can get paid for, and what

---

15 Sinek, S. (2017). Find Your Why: A Practical Guide for Discovering Purpose for You and Your Team. *Penguin Books.*
16 García, H., Miralles, F., & Cleary, H. (2018). Ikigai: The Japanese Secret to a Long and Happy Life. *Waterville, ME: Thorndike Press Large Print.*

Mutual Vision: Why you're in your role

the world needs, depicted in the figure below.[17] For these authors, passion is the blend of what we love and what we're good at, but it isn't necessarily something that the world needs or will pay us to do.

I do like the four arenas, and it's helpful to think in these terms for determining your vision for your life. However, they separate the definitions of vocation and profession based on whether what you get paid for is something the world needs, or something you're good at. It starts to resemble an unnecessary exercise in semantics. I also find the authors' definition of mission too restrictive. But I'll address that in the next chapter.

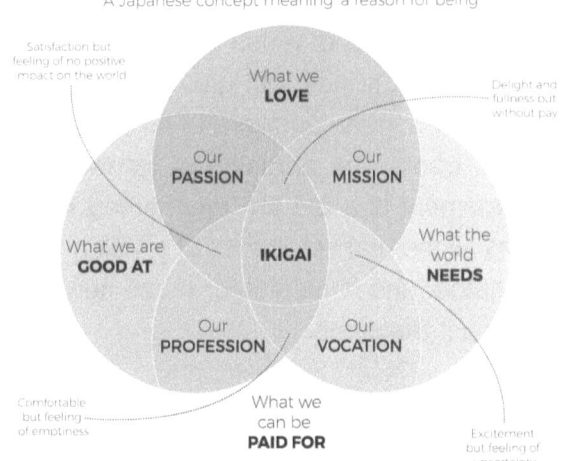

---

17 Law, T. (2018, April 05). How Ikigai can be applied to early-stage companies. Retrieved from https://wearehowdoi.com/news/2018/6/1/how-ikigai-can-be-applied-to-early-stage-companies

Moustafa Hamwi from PassionPreneur calls vision your "Passion." Hamwi writes that "Passion is consistently doing what you love, what you are good at, and what is of value to the world."[18] This take on the perfect job paradigm collapses the two Ikigai concepts of *what is needed*, and *what you can get paid for* into one idea called *value to the world*, and adds it to the definition of passion. Yet, Hamwi still seeks to find career activity in the common concept blend of skills, talent, and market demand. What you do well might not be what you love to do, but what you love to do might not pay enough to live.

So, to Hamwi, the balance is in finding something that sits amid those three arenas, assuming that for what is of value to the world, someone will pay you to do it. Passion is something that is found within yourself, by conducting an inventory of the activities that give you life, and looking for common themes in the answers to 40 questions that he provides in his book. The phrasing of Hamwi's version of a Passion Statement is a tad too regimented for my liking, but it contains all the main elements of a vision and mission statement together and is helpful for those new to this, so I recommend it just the same.

Rick Warren, founding pastor of Saddleback Church in California, and author of *The Purpose Driven Life* (which has sold more than 50 million copies), calls it your "Purpose." For Warren, purpose isn't something that you

---

18 Hamwi, M. (2019).

find by looking inside yourself as Hamwi suggests, but rather something for which you were created, which you discover in service to others. Your purpose is discovered by aligning yourself with God, and His intention for your life. He says, "You are not an assembly line product, mass produced without thought. You are a custom-designed, one-of-a-kind, original masterpiece."[19] In Warren's view, a life's purpose isn't for you to design so much as to discover. He encourages readers to think of their life in terms of their death, with an intent toward building up a life that matters long after one's last breath.

Warren's version is fatalistic in that it is not determined by an individual, but by God and only recognized by an individual. Yet, his *Purpose Driven Life* has sold some 50+ million copies and may be the best-selling non-fiction book of all time, so perhaps, it's smart to consider the wisdom of the crowd on this definition.

Oprah Winfrey refers to this concept as a "Calling." She tells a story from 1978, when she was demoted from a news anchor to the talk show, People are Talking. While she used to drag herself to work on the news, on the talk show, she found life and energy in her work. "That day, my 'job' ended and my calling began," she writes. "When you pay attention to what feeds your energy, you move in the direction of the life for which you were intended. Trust that the Universe has

---

19 Warren, R. (2002). The Purpose-Driven Life: What on Earth Am I Here For? *Grand Rapids, Michigan: Zondervan.*

a bigger, wider, deeper dream for you than you could ever imagine for yourself."[20]

Writing your vision is a step of acceptance in your articulation of that dream, that Calling. Again, in her fairly fatalistic view, Winfrey's Calling is something to be responded to rather than determined by the individual. This can be too extrinsic for some readers.

I highlight these authors only to show you that there are different ways of thinking about a vision statement. Every author has their own twist to what is essentially the same concept: your personal description of your future best-life scenario. Whether or not you believe in God might influence how much of your vision is determined by you and how much of it is discovered by you, but the outcome is essentially the same, you'll describe what you, at your best, will aim for in the future.

Keep in mind, Reader, that the only person to whom your vision statement needs to be meaningful, is you. Long or short doesn't matter. It doesn't have to start with a particular word or set of words. It can strike a balance between ambiguity on the things you don't want to be too rigid about, and clarity on the things you do. You are the only person who has to read this statement and find meaning in it, so

---

[20] Winfrey, O. (2019). *The Path Made Clear: Discovering Your Life's Direction and Purpose*. *London: Melcher.*

write it in a way that's clear to you, even if it's not clear to anyone else.

You don't have to use the words, *vision, passion, purpose*, or *calling* to describe your vision. Call it whatever you like. I'll call it a vision statement in this book because it's common vernacular in business, because it implies something you see ahead of you, and because we have to agree to call it something.

My first focused attempt at writing my vision statement was in 2006. I was 30, and my professor called it a Personal Life Mandate (PLM). The PLM format is longer, and highly purposeful in language. Mine used phrases like, "I will … " to indicate intent, and this may be helpful to some younger readers. I was a lot more religious then than I am now, and it shows in the wording of my vision:

> My life purpose is to **engage other cultures** through dialogue, leadership training, and formal teaching in academic settings. I will also **encourage people to live according to the life example of Jesus**. I will **begin new organizations**, which will find new leadership in those I **personally mentor**. My influence with **high level leaders** will tend to exceed the authority of the positions I will hold. I will **be transient**, and **accept personal risk** for the advancement of my purpose. I will be both cunning and gentle, and pray that **God will bless my family**.

Yikes, I wrote that?! Wow. Uh, this is embarrassing. I don't suppose I can go back on this whole transparency / I'll show you mine thing … can I?

Ok, well, first of all, it's a bit wordy, but I guess the major ideas are clear. I haven't read this in about 15 years, so it's interesting for me to excavate it now. I liked to travel, learn languages, start companies, pursue academics, and network with and develop leaders. I had a pretty high tolerance for risk and ambiguity. I valued my faith and my family. I wanted to see outcomes in all of these areas. I suppose that's pretty good clarity for a 30-year-old.

In subsequent years, I'm happy to say that I've more or less stuck to the plan. I moved from Estonia to Yemen, then to the UAE. I added Arabic to my list of competencies. I still travel a lot, enjoy networking, and I'm heavily focused on leadership development in my work. I've started three other companies of my own and worked entrepreneurially in a dozen more. I've received four post-graduate degrees and have a couple of dozen publications to my name.

My religion has become less important to me, but my faith remains the same, and has become much more tangible to me. My commitment to family has become clearer since being divorced, remarrying, and taking on a broader family network. I also stopped calling it a Personal Life Mandate and started calling it a vision statement, because it was easier to write and it meshed with what I was doing for companies, and for no other reason at all. I personally don't care what you call your vision statement.

Knowing so well who I was at that time, and making decisions in line with this vision, gives me a sense of pride in myself and my work. My current, shorter version (see p. 75) is, to me, a more succinct and simplified version of the older one. And I have to agree with Simon Sinek that shorter and clearer is better for me. As I get older, I'm becoming clearer about who I am and what I stand for. I hope you do too.

I've shown you mine … now show me yours. Who are you and what do you stand for?

Your Vision

We'll start the process of designing your life by first imagining the day of your death. If you're an experienced writer, then perhaps you'd like to open up your tablet and start writing.

Who is speaking at your funeral?

_____

What kinds of people are in attendance?

_____

What kinds of things did you do in life?

_____

_____

_____

_____

_____

_____

What kinds of things did you care about most?

_____

_____

_____

_____

_____

_____

_____

What are the artifacts you've left behind? These could be tangible objects such as artwork, books, property, products, buildings, or intangible artifacts such as values that you've intentionally reproduced in your children, students, or employees.

_____

_____

_____

_____

_____

_____

Now, let's take a crack at this without any more of my definitions or meddling. You don't need any more resources than those you already have. Start with keywords and ideas and go from there. I recommend that you write in pencil, because you'll go through a dozen edits before you become happy with it.

What is your vision? If everything goes well, what would you like to achieve in your life?

_____

_____

_____

_____

_____

_____

_____

_____

_____

_____

As I've said above, words are intensely meaningful, but in this case, they're for an audience of one. What you've written above only needs to be meaningful to you. Also, it's probably going to go through a few more iterations before you're happy with it. And you might change it several times over the years. So, don't be too critical of yourself on the wording right now.

Just as a recent example, in 2018, I had an embarrassing moment in front of an executive committee (EXCO) for a large corporate client of mine. I was working with the EXCO to establish the new vision, mission, and values for a group of companies within a second-generation family company with professionalized management. Amazing people. Anyway, it's my policy not to develop the vision, mission, and values for a company unless I am doing it for each of the individuals at the table at the same time. And as a part of that process, to build transparency and trust in the room, I show them mine.

I clicked over the slide of my personal vision statement, which read:

vision
To be an honorable father, a polymath scholar, and a globally recognized business strategist.

About six months before this meeting, I had gotten divorced. It was a particularly painful experience for me. During my healing process, I had brought out my vision statement, and, having removed the ring from my finger, edited out the term, "and husband," from my vision. I was angry, and hurt, and it was the first edit to my vision statement in several years.

Months later, I read it aloud to this executive committee. And then, I must have been staring at the slide for a few seconds too long, because the CEO of the Family Office asked me awkwardly:

"Dr. Corrie, is everything ok?"

"Sorry, what?"

"Is everything ok? Are you alright?"

"Sorry Ziad, yes. Well, no. There used to be another term here. It used to read 'honorable father and husband.' But I took out the husband part after my divorce earlier this year."

"So, what's the problem? You're not married anymore."

"The problem is that I miss being a husband. I enjoyed it. Having a divorce under my belt, I'm questioning how talented I was at it, but I certainly prefer being a husband to not being a husband. I definitely intend to do that again."

"Well, maybe you should put it back in then."

So, in a very unprofessional and unpolished move, I popped my laptop out of presentation mode right there in the meeting room, and in front of a team of distinguished strangers, I reinstated the phrase: "honorable father *and husband*." I felt relieved. I apologized and we moved on.

But from that day, I saw myself as a wifeless husband, and that simple change of my meaningful words changed my frame of mind. I was already in love with Nicole, and so I became more focused, more intent, and it changed the way I thought about, treated, and made future plans with her. Thanks to her, I am a husband again now, and very glad for that. She is my last true love, and I will continue to work daily to earn the 'honorable' part of that visionary title.

I suppose you'll have to ask her how well I'm doing in that department.

I have the privilege of working with a number of remarkable companies every year on their meaningful words for their corporate community. One of the advantages is that I get to facilitate the shaping of words that govern thousands of employees in dozens of companies. One of the drawbacks is that I don't have a corporate community of my own that I can connect half of my life with. I'm not an employee, which has benefits and drawbacks.

Employees are members of corporate communities. And those corporate communities are managed by meaningful texts, which often include some form of vision, mission, and values statements. These tenets govern the agreed upon economic project that is comprised of half of the human experience of every employee in that community, every day that they work there. That's a huge opportunity to create meaning in peoples' lives.

Mutual Vision

Let's quickly review some important truths …

1. You're not a machine. As a human, your best strategy for survival on the planet is to do so as a member in a team of people who are competing for resources on the planet by playing an economic game together.

That's very likely how you're making a living right now.
2. You're not a victim, and you're not a slave. You are in the role you're in (or not in) as a direct result of every decision you have ever made, both good and bad. Sometimes things worked out for you and sometimes they didn't, but you were an active participant in the process that led you to where you are now.
3. You're not an idiot. You are doing what you're doing because you believe that it's the best, fastest, most effective way available to you for you to reach your personal vision and accomplish your personal goals. If you knew of a better way, you'd be doing that instead.

So, you're not a machine, not a victim, and not an idiot. Which means that you can take ownership of the role you're in right now. If you don't like your role, or your boss, or your company, you have options. You can change your job, or change your mind. Your call.

But before you hand in your resignation in order to follow your newly-formed personal vision, let's take a quick look at why you're in the company you're in now, and what role that has already played in leading you towards your definition of a meaningful life. We're going to need your vision statement, and the vision (or similar) statement of your organization. If your company doesn't have one, that's ok, pick one from a company that you aspire to work with in the future. Trust me, it will help. Go ahead and write the company vision here:

Mutual Vision: Why you're in your role

_____

_____

_____

_____

Now, let's park that for a bit so that I can introduce you to James. I mentioned him briefly in the introduction to this book. He also wrote the foreword, which most readers skip by ... so if you skipped the foreword, now is a great time to read it for context on what's coming next.

He's a real person, but James is not his real name. James works for Al Masaood Group (AMG) of Companies in Abu Dhabi, UAE. Like me, he's in his 40s. And having gone through my 'Business is Personal' program at AMG, he has established his personal vision, mission, values, and goals. James has given me permission to use his words and those of his corporate community to illustrate the idea of mutual strategy for you.

You see, James has dedicated half of his life to an economic project based out of Abu Dhabi that feeds not only his family, but many other families as well. He is working with a massive team of people to compete for resources on the planet. You can imagine two thousand people, with two thousand personal vision statements, all intersecting for half of their lives each day on a project governed by a single vision statement:

AMG's vision
Growing Together, Delivering Value,
Embracing Heritage

Rather than a full sentence, AMG decided to go with a triad of phrases for their corporate vision. Which is totally fine, by the way. Why? Because it's meaningful to them. It doesn't need to be more complex than that.

For his personal vision statement, James had chosen a more traditional approach:

James' vision
Be an approachable and dynamic leader
and friend, constantly inspiring and
empowering those around me.

James had, somewhere in the midpoint of his life, found himself dedicating half of his human experience to an economic project that used the three phrases above to describe its collective intention for the future. That's a really important discovery for James. Clearly, if half of his life each day is meant to be invested in growing together, delivering value, and embracing heritage, he'd need to be able to describe how half of his life contributes to that vision. So, I asked him:

"James, what meaning do you find in the vision of AMG?"

"What do you mean?"

"Well, you've dedicated half of your life to this project for a while, so you must be able to see yourself in those words somehow. When you look at those three phrases, what do you see? How does your vision align with the vision of the community that helps you feed your family?"

And this was his reply (paraphrased):

James' vision	AMG's vision
Approachable and dynamic leader and friend	= Growing Together
Constantly inspiring	= Delivering Value
Empowering those around me	= Embracing Heritage

For James, once he had the words of his vision written down, he could see directly how his own life was contributing to the vision of his economic community, and how the meaningful words of his economic community were also meaningfully connected to his own. The fun thing about this is that all of this meaning, all of this added value, was created in James' mind.

In James' company, I had more than 120 executives and top managers go through this process. Without fail, each one of them found personal meaning in the community's words.

Every. Single. Person.

But the company's statements resonated uniquely for every different employee. Others in James' company saw and found different connections between their personal visions and the vision of the organization. And each of those connections was meaningful to the individual that created and described it. So you see, there's no right or wrong answer to the question of what you find meaningful in your community's vision. It's entirely up to you.

What words or concepts in your company's vision statement resonate with you? You don't have to connect to all of it, but since it's governing about half of your life every day, it's unlikely that you will connect to none of it.

Your vision	Your Company's vision

Mutual Vision: Why you're in your role

1. What fresh meaning can you discover in comparing your vision with that of your company?
2. Can you see how you being in this organization is contributing towards the organization's vision?
3. Can you see how you being in this organization is contributing towards your own personal vision?
4. Why are you in the job role you're in now?
5. Can you see the path from where you used to be through where you are now to where you want to be in the future?

Remember, your job role isn't your whole life, but it is about half of it. So, you should be able to find meaning when you look through the lenses of both your vision and your company's vision. The quality of half of your life depends on your ability to find meaning in your work.

Also, you're not an idiot or a slave, so you should be able to see how your participation in this economic community is helping you achieve your personal vision.

What to Do if You Can't Find Meaning

In my experience, having done this with hundreds of managers in dozens of companies, I have not yet found a single person who couldn't find meaning in the meaningful words that govern the half of their life that they are spending at work. So, if you have taken a fair look at your vision, and a fair look at the vision of your organization, and you can't find meaning, it's for one of these three reasons:

1. I didn't explain it well enough.
2. You didn't understand it well enough.
3. You don't want to find meaning at work.

In the first case, that's my mistake. I've been teaching these principles for years, but this is the first time that I've written them down in a book. It's certainly possible that I've done a less than adequate job of clarifying the concepts for you. If this is the case, I apologize. Please feel free to stop reading this book as it'll become much more frustrating for you in subsequent chapters. I'm glad we had a chance to interact, and I hope that in some small way, this experience has improved the quality of your life.

In the second case, here's a synopsis of some preceding thoughts to help:

- All humans find words meaningful, and all humans in groups are organized by meaningful words.
- The meaningful words that organize companies are an example of how humans organize themselves.
- The meaningful words of your organization are an example of how words have been used by your company's leaders to organize and give meaning to half of your own personal life.
- The meaning you find in the overlap between your vision and that of your corporate community is entirely unique to you.

The third case is the most likely though. If you can't find meaning, chances are that you are resisting it. Humans are highly skilled at finding meaning in things, and it's a low hanging fruit for you to find meaning in your own life. If you are resisting the natural human instinct to find meaning at work, then it's probably for one of these reasons:

1. You are not proud of what your company does.
2. You feel underappreciated there.
3. You feel hurt or marginalized by your co-workers.
4. You feel trapped in your job.

Does that sound about right? You're not a victim and you're not a slave, so if you can't find meaning in half of your life, then you need to either change your job, or change your mind.

Change Your Job

This is the hard road. You'll have to end your relationship with the economic community that you're currently committing half of your life to. It's a big decision. Ending any kind of relationship and leaving any kind of community incurs a cost. But it's worth it to find a path towards more meaning in your life. Besides, if you continue to take up space in a community that you're not aligned to, then you're robbing someone else out there of a potential place in a community that is meaningful to them. And that's mean. So, don't be mean.

I encourage you to take the high road here. Leave in a way that you are proud of yourself. Don't steal time or resources from your current community on your way out. Do your work faithfully, and to the best of your ability while you are making plans to shift communities. And when you are looking for a new role, pay more attention to the meaningful words of the communities you are considering to move to. You'll be dedicating half of your life each day to a new set of corporate goals, so be intentional about making sure you find meaning in them before you accept an interview.

Change Your Mind

This is the easier road. You can work on your relationships with your manager and co-workers. It's beyond the scope of this book, but here are three things you can try:

1. Make more oxytocin. Helping behavior among humans is both contagious and addictive. Humans can't help but react favorably to small acts of kindness. When humans see humans helping others, they feel obligated as members of their own communities to help others as well. Small consistent changes in this direction will benefit those you help, and it will produce more oxytocin in your own brain, which will help you feel more connected at work. Don't try to connect with the company, just connect with the seven people that you work closely with.
2. Humanize your colleagues. Every human is a little bit insecure on the inside. Everyone in your company is dedicating half of their lives to an economic project with no guarantee of lifetime success. Try to empathize with your co-workers and your boss. See them as people with hopes and fears just like you, and with personal visions for their own lives that they are also struggling to achieve.
3. "Momentize" your work. Look for opportunities to make your work more meaningful, by setting up and achieving small wins. Get involved in your company's corporate social responsibility initiatives, improve

a process, or learn a new skill. When you achieve a few smaller meaningful things, you'll find new paths towards contributing to the community in a way that's more meaningful to you.

Ultimately, you are designing your own life, and your work makes up about half of it. You can't ignore it or distance yourself from it. You've got you here. Now, it's time for clarity and reckoning. Whether you love your job or hate it, it's a big part of you, and it is leading you in the direction of your personal vision for your life. Valuing your work starts with valuing yourself. And now that we have some idea of where you want to go in the future, we need to look at how you would like to get there.

CHAPTER 5

Mutual Mission: How we're getting it done

My Mission

It was the middle of winter in Estonia. There was a foot-high layer of snow on the ground, and we were bundled up in our warmest coats and boots as we marched out onto the ice with a chainsaw at the Bishop's house outside of Tallinn. It wasn't cold, not by Estonian standards, maybe -10 degrees Celsius. But the ice covering the small homemade lake was several inches thick. We would have to cut a hole in that ice if we were going to jump into the water below to cool down. Chainsaws are handy for that.

After cutting a three-foot-wide hole in the ice, we pushed the core we had cut out down and watched it slip away under the ice sheet. Then, we went back into the house to get naked, and grab a beer, before heading into the most holy place for conversations with Estonians: the sauna. Rod, Dave, and I made regular visits to Bishop Mart's house, to sit in the sauna with him and have him challenge us on our lives, loves, and pursuits of meaning.

At 110 degrees Celsius (230 degrees Fahrenheit), the Estonian sauna is a perfect environment for encouraging transparency and trust. You have to be naked when you enter, and so there I was once again, nude as the day I was born, sitting with my colleagues and mentors. We dumped a mug of water on the hot rocks in the sauna so that a pillar of steam rose up to the ceiling, and curled down like an angry hand that slapped us on our backs, turning breathing into a conscious exercise. After a minute, the cloud subsided enough for us to be able to talk again.

We rarely talked about sports, or the news. Instead, in a room of naked men, it was appropriate to bare our souls. We talked about our lives, our sense of calling towards a higher purpose, and the means by which we were each achieving what we believed God had put us on the planet to do. For me that meant charity work, youth education, starting small businesses, and eventually going back to school. Rod and Dave joined Mart in encouraging me to return to university and finish a master's degree in something leadership oriented.

When it got too hot for us to remain in the sauna, we would take a quiet walk out of the house into the snow. Dawn (my first wife) remarked to me how awkwardly entertaining it was for her to be seated with the wives in the kitchen, facing the window to the backyard when the motion sensor light would activate and she would unwittingly look up to catch a glimpse of a train of pasty white bums marching through the snow to the lake. And one by one, we dropped fully into the water through the hole we'd cut, springing up to life again onto the snow-covered ice.

It takes a while to cool down once you've spent a good long time in a sauna, so we'd sometimes make anatomically correct snow angels before sitting down together at the table outside for a while. There we would have a glass of port, a fine cigar, and continue our conversation. When we got too cold, we'd park our cigars for a bit and march back to the sauna for another cycle of therapy.

I loved those conversations. Nothing was off limits. The vulnerability of our complete nakedness fueled moments of open reflection on new and exciting ways to live out our lives. It was in those conversations that I first dreamt up a media production company called Eye Candy, and a sound equipment rental/party production company called Ear Candy. It was in those conversations that I was most challenged to see myself with something that I could develop, craft, and hone in relationships with other leaders, with my family, and with God. And it was in those conversations that I became aware of my learning addiction.

I read ferociously and took my learning into the sauna so that I could think out loud with others about how I was doing what I felt called to do. And through the tempering of fire and ice, and the candid words of correction and encouragement from my closest friends, I learned my best practices: learning, teaching, thinking, writing, public speaking, skill development, organizational design, entrepreneurship, and personal character development. What a blessing it was to have had that clarity way back in the early 2000s.

My mentors at that time were Alan, Mart, Rod, Dave, Joyce, Darcy, Kory, and Dawn. Each of them pushed me to do something that I mistakenly thought I had no inclination for at the time, but turned out to be one of the most fun things I've ever done: academic research.

My mission
To pursue excellence in my academic, professional, and home life through the disciplines of personal character development, dynamic thinking, and relentless curiosity.

That's my mission today. And this too has evolved from a mess of content into a more meaningful set of words that I'll share with you below. Here, we will turn our attention to the mission statement, what it is, how it differs from a vision statement, and how you can write one of your own powerful enough to govern your decisions.

What's a Mission Statement?

The mission statement is the most difficult and most confused concept in corporate strategy. Some authors find no difference in the definitions of a mission and vision. Some propose a mission to be ambiguous and aspirational, others to be so crystal clear that there is little room for either interpretation or inspiration. There are a lot of different versions of this, but they all tend towards the same outcome: describing your methodology for success. In brief, your vision statement brings into words a picture of what you want to achieve in the future, and your mission statement brings into words the means by which you plan to achieve it. It adds a small but meaningful layer of clarity to your overall life strategy. For our purposes here, we'll call it a mission statement; but once again, I don't care what you call it. It only needs to be meaningful to you.

In my work with both individuals and companies, I use the illustration of a journey. Vision is an idea of a destination, and mission, the means of transportation. If the vision is to get to London, the mission might be a boat, plane, camel, bicycle, and/or car. It might include a commitment to using only a certain kind of fuel such as petrol, or solar energy, or human power. It might reference a quality of the experience, such as speed, comfort, or photographing key places along the way. The vision is the intended destination, and the mission is the intended means of reaching it.

In the original history of the word, mission outlined the journey of someone sent for a purpose. The vision might have been a treaty with a foreign kingdom, but the mission, in its primary meaning, would have been the emissary's journey to deliver a letter with terms for negotiation between two kings. It describes the act of 'being sent', or the 'going and doing' part of achieving a great vision.

In 1961, one of John F. Kennedy's visions was that the US, "should commit itself to achieving the goal, before this decade is out, of landing a man on the Moon and returning him safely to the Earth." That vision was ultimately managed, step by step, through the NASA office called Mission Control. They managed the resources and the means by which the vision was achieved.

Simon Sinek calls the mission layer, the "How" statement. It's the second layer of his Golden Circle. In the center is "Why," followed by "How," and then eventually "What." We'll get to the "What" later. For now, we'll look at the How, which Sinek describes in a corporate setting as your Unique Selling Proposition (USP) or differentiating value proposition. For an individual, this could be as simple as your job title.[21] You might have a lofty ambition for your life in your vision statement, but your way of getting there could include a specific career path, such as being an accountant, medical doctor, violinist, graphic artist, or shoe salesman.

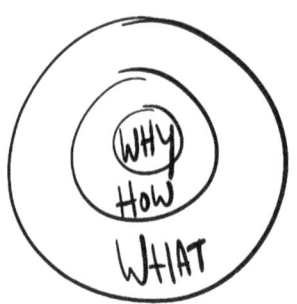

---

21 Sinek, S (2017).

Management guru Peter Drucker writes: "A mission cannot be impersonal; it has to have deep meaning, be something you believe in – something you know is right. A fundamental responsibility of leadership is to make sure that everybody knows the mission, understands it, lives it."[22] There is some overlap with vision in the definitions of mission as described by Peter Drucker and Jim Collins, but the core message is the same. It's a principle-based description of the behavior that leads to accomplishing the organization's, or an individual's, core purpose for existence.

Back in the 1980s, the idea of mission statements for companies was just becoming mainstream. Management academics studied the composition and impact of emerging corporate mission statements. One study by Pearce and David identified no less than eight components of a corporate mission statement.

1. Targeted customers and markets;
2. Principal products and services;
3. Geographic domain;
4. Core technologies;
5. Commitment to survival, growth, and profitability;
6. Key elements in the company philosophy;

---

22 Drucker, P. F., & Collins, J. (2008). *The Five Most Important Questions You Will Ever Ask About Your Organization.* New York: Leader to Leader Institute.

7. The company's self-concept; and
8. The firm's desired public image.[23]

Yikes! I'm glad we're not in the 80s anymore. These elements are far too restrictive for my taste. Of course, if it's meaningful for you to do so, please feel free to include an individualized version of all these items in your personal mission statement. But if not, don't bother. Seriously, it's much too restrictive.

Collins and Porras get much closer to the heart of the matter, noting that,

> "most mission statements are terribly ineffective as a compelling, guiding force. In fact, most corporate statements we've encountered – be they called mission, vision, purpose, philosophy, credo, or the company way – are of little value. They don't have the intended effect. They don't grab people in the gut and motivate them to work toward a common end. They don't focus attention. They don't galvanize people to put forth their best efforts toward a compelling goal. They don't mean something to people all up and down the organization. In fact, they are usually nothing more than a boring stream of words."[24]

---

23 Pearce, J. A., & David, F. (1987). *Corporate Mission Statements: The Bottom Line.* Academy of Management Perspectives, *1(2)*, 109-115.

24 Collins, J. C., & Porras, J. I. (1991). *Organizational Vision and Visionary Organizations.* California Management Review, *34(1)*, 30-52.

So instead, they offer their own definition: "A mission is a clear and compelling goal that serves to unify an organization's efforts. An effective mission must stretch and challenge the organization, yet be achievable."[25] The authors call this the Big Hairy Audacious Goal (BHAG). For me, this is not enough to fully define a mission statement, but I really like the language of the BHAG. The BHAG might be better described as the vision and mission together.

A mission statement, whether for an organization or for an individual, should bring some clarity to the means by which the vision will be achieved, but it shouldn't be in strict goal language just as yet. We'll deal with that in Chapter 7. Instead, it should outline the kinds of activities, the things that you will do, to achieve your vision. If your vision includes becoming a world-renowned musician, then the mission should include the kind of music you will pursue, whether as a soloist or in a band, or in an orchestra. It might include your commitment to practice and future learning, and to the kinds of venues where you will exhibit your craft.

Moustafa Hamwi includes a set of 40 questions in his book that are helpful for finding clarity in the kinds of things you generally enjoy doing, and the kinds of things you do naturally.[26] I like this approach, since I agree that the best way for a person to achieve their vision is to do it by means that come naturally to them, and that they enjoy doing. It will

---

25 Collins, J. C., & Porras, J. I. (1991).
26 Hamwi, M. (2019).

be very empowering for you as well to see that the kinds of activities you are good at and enjoy, will be your best methodology for achieving your vision.

Ask yourself:

1. What do I enjoy doing?
2. What do I do better than others?
3. What do I focus on doing to make sure I'm always headed towards my vision?

The operative word in each of these questions is the word, "do." What will you do? It's the 'doing' that we will concentrate on here, not the seeing as we did in your vision statement above.

When I tried to describe this back in 2006, when I was 30 years old, I wrote down a lot of information. I was young, a zealot in my faith, and still learning what my best methodologies were. I'm a little cautious to share this with you, since some of this is not how I see myself now. But in the interest of transparency, here's the methodology section of what I then called my Personal Life Mandate (PLM):

> My effective methodologies will include teaching, most often by informal means. I will earn the right to speak and write with authority by matching my lifestyle to my teaching, and preparing my materials well. I will continue to study literature, to be well informed, to seek input from naïve and dissonant voices in my

learning, and to articulate new understanding of and to the Christian worldview.

I believe God's favor will also afford me opportunities of informal influence with one or two at a time, especially with high level leaders. I will anticipate that God will fill my mouth with wisdom beyond my learning when I am in a position of such influence and have the opportunity to speak.

I will be involved in direct intercultural work with high-level leaders, often involving great risk and/or sacrifice. I will trust God to provide my financial, practical, and security needs. I will move quickly, though not neglecting my body's need for rest. I will run the good race, neither walking nor crawling when I am able to do otherwise. I will try new things, to pioneer my consulting practice in new venues with creative methods. Though my work will be transient and highly dynamic, I will have a good sense at the beginning of what the fruit of each endeavor should look like. I intend to personally train replacements for each position I hold.

I will submit myself to mentoring, both in accountability through disclosure, and in vulnerability through submission to directives. I will choose my mentors intentionally, and allow myself to be chosen by others as a mentor.

As often as possible, I will lead through a team of which I am a part, as I have found team leadership to be an effective multiplier of my efforts. I will also aim to positively influence organizations of which I am a part through upstream leadership. I will exhort those above me positionally to greater spiritual leadership and responsibility.

That's a lot of words. Far too many, in fact, compared with my current one, "To pursue excellence in my academic, professional, and home life through the disciplines of personal character development, dynamic thinking, and relentless curiosity."

But it was helpful at that time for me to have a longer description of what made me effective in my work. You'll see that my dominant methodologies included reading, writing, leadership development, personal development, mentoring, creativity, risk-taking, transparency, pioneering, entrepreneurship, teams, and trust in God.

In my most recent version of my mission, I have consolidated all of these pursuits into the three most basic activities I could think of: character development, thinking, and curiosity. It might seem strange to some that I would include curiosity as an activity, for example; but as something I'm really great at and enjoy, being intentionally curious has become a core methodology.

Reading and writing are not my core means of achieving success, but curiosity and thinking are. Reading and writing are just kinds of input and output. They might just as soon be watching Ted Talks (input) and public speaking (output). But it took me another decade or so to identify that, and to abbreviate my mission into a more succinct and accurate meaning for me.

I also clarified my three core domains in my most recent mission. I've outlined my academic, professional, and home life as the three major arenas in which I want to concentrate my efforts. This is clearer for me now and adds a lot of meaning. So, when you draft your own mission statement, go ahead and make it as wordy as you want to. When things become clearer to you over time, you can consolidate terms and reduce the number of words that you need to describe your overall mission.

Your Mission

Peter Drucker once said: "Your mission should fit on a t-shirt." That's a good benchmark, but I'm a leadership writer, and it took me a full decade to get my mission to that level of succinctness, so don't put too much pressure on yourself. We'll get you to a draft of a mission statement now, but instead of concentrating on how few words you can cram it into, I want you to concentrate on making sure that nothing meaningful (for you) is left out.

It will help to flip back to the section called *You Are Your Job*, in Chapter 1 (page 25/30), in which you listed your current social roles. Read them out. Then try to group them into domains in your life. What are the 3-5 major areas in your life that you would like to focus on? Write them down here:

_____

_____

_____

_____

_____

Now, ask yourself: do all of my roles fit into the domains I've just listed? Are there any roles I've missed? Are there domains I've left out? If so, go ahead and incorporate them.

Let's switch gears for a moment and do a brief inventory of the things that you are good at and enjoy doing.

What do you do better than others? What are the skills you have that are valuable to the world around you? In this next exercise, I want you to write down ten things that you're really good at. This should include some of the skills that got you into your current work role, such as accounting, graphic design, management, etc.

Ten things I'm Good at:

_____   _____

_____   _____

_____   _____

_____   _____

_____   _____

Now what do you like to do? What energizes you? What activities bring joy? List your top ten here. Don't move on until you have at least ten things.

Ten things I Enjoy:

_____   _____

_____   _____

_____   _____

_____   _____

Don't limit yourself to things you're good at, to the neglect of things you enjoy. My list would include CrossFit and yoga, even though I'm not really amazing at either of them. Same with karaoke. After a couple of malted beverages, I've been known, on occasion, to grab a microphone and wail out my own take on Bohemian Rhapsody. But enjoying it doesn't mean I'll ever be a lead singer on stage.

Now take a minute to enjoy the moment. Look at that list you've created! That's amazing. You're good at all of those things, and you know it! Pat yourself on the back for a second, smile, and recognize your strengths in these areas. Good job for good job!

Ok, we're on a roll now. But the next one's going to be a little tougher.

Remember how I added the academic domain to my mission while smoking cigars naked in sub-zero temperatures with a group of colleagues and mentors? I wouldn't have thought of academics if those around me hadn't pushed me to pursue it. It was an arena that opened up at the prompting of others, and has now become a core domain for me. It helped me to hone in on my mission. The point is, sometimes we're good at things we don't recognize in ourselves. For this, we need to listen to our community.

Take out your phone now. I want you to choose two people you work with, and two others you don't work with but who know you quite well. Now write a simple message to them, something like this:

> "Hi. I'm working on a personal project at the moment and I would really value your input on something. What have you noticed that I'm really good at? What particular skills or abilities would you say I have? Just 2 or 3 things would be great."

Feel free to change the wording to match your own voice. But keep in mind that since we're working on a mission statement, the operative word here is "do." We're looking for input from your community on what you are good at "doing."

Email or text them your message.

Things Person 1 _____ says I'm good at:

_____

_____

_____

Things Person 2 _____ says I'm good at:

_____

_____

_____

Things Person 3 _____ says I'm good at:

_____

_____

_____

Things Person 4 _____ says I'm good at:

_____

_____

_____

While you're waiting for their responses, I want you to pay attention to the sense of anxiety that might come from doing this kind of feedback exercise. The reason you're nervous while waiting for these replies is that community is important, and words are meaningful. You're human, after all. Embrace that.

As humans, to survive, we need to be in a community, and we all have an innate desire to make meaningful contributions to our communities. We sometimes worry that even the people closest to us won't see or value our contributions, and if so, that we're less valuable to our community than we'd hoped we were.

Also, none of these people will be able to see your intentions or motivations. All they will ever have to describe you is your behavior. What if your intentions and your behaviors don't line up the way that you want them to? What if they see things in your behaviors that you didn't intend? That can be a bit disconcerting.

Remember Ahmad the yeller from Chapter 1? He didn't think of himself as someone who yelled at his employees, but that's what he did. He found out from me that he was exactly the kind of person that yells at his employees. The same principle works in reverse, we can find out from others that we're good at things we didn't recognize. This happened to me personally. Remember earlier in this chapter when I told you how my mentors pushed me to get into academics? That's because others saw skills and abilities in me that I didn't see in myself. You never fully know what you're good at until you receive the right feedback.

So finally, what if they see a skill or ability in you that you hadn't seen before? A freebie! What will that mean for your sense of identity? How might that broaden or challenge your view of what you are capable of or good at?

Many of these concerns may be in the back of your mind when you ask friends for their feedback. They're all normal human concerns. Just remind yourself that these people only see small sections of your life. They see a small collection of your behaviors, and absolutely none of your intentions. So, go easy on them. They're human too. They won't be 100% correct, nor will they be 100% incorrect. Their feedback will provide an opportunity for you to see things about yourself that you might not have noticed.

Try to wait now until you've received feedback from at least three people. It might take a day or two, so this is a good time for you to put this book down for a bit. Maybe catch up on a Netflix show you've been meaning to watch. I like documentaries. My wife and I occasionally take a whole day and binge-watch a limited series documentary together over a couple of bottles of wine and some takeaway food. Good times.

You should now have three lists:

1. Things you do that you are good at
2. Things that you enjoy doing, and
3. Things that other people think you're good at

Once you have that, we can move on.

Take your pencil or pen, and circle three things from each of the three lists that are the most meaningful to you. In each list, circle the three words or phrases that you best connect with. The ones that give you life when you read them, the words that make you proud to be you. The activities without which your life would have significantly less meaning. Go ahead and do that. You should end up with around nine meaningful sets of words. But if it's more or less, that's ok too. Write them down here:

The three most meaningful things that I enjoy doing:

_____

_____

_____

The three most meaningful things that I'm good at doing:

_____

_____

_____

The three most meaningful things that other people say I'm good at doing:

_____

_____

_____

Now recall the 3-5 major domains in your life (Page 114) that you want to focus on:

_____

_____

_____

_____

_____

This is the beginning of your mission statement. Go ahead and take a shot at drafting those things into a set of meaningful words that describe your best approach for achieving your life vision. Include your major domains, your best skills and abilities, and activities that you exhibit that move you in that direction. It can be as long or short as you like, but my advice is that you should make sure not to leave anything out that's meaningful to you.

My Mission Statement:

_____

_____

_____

_____

_____

_____

_____

_____

_____

_____

Ok, now you have a meaningful description of the things that you DO that can help you reach your vision. But let's not forget that half or more of everything you do is at work, in your social role as a member of an economic community. The next step in the process is to see how what you do with half of your life contributes to your corporate community's conception of what you are all doing together.

Mutual Mission

The talents and skills that make up your best methodology for achieving your personal vision are the same ones that make you successful in your career. Think about it. You spend half of your life at work, so what you do best will definitely come out in that environment and move you forward. You've spent your whole life getting better and better at certain activities and behaviors that not only contribute to your vision, but are also recognized by your corporate community in a way that makes you valuable to them.

You're neither an idiot nor a victim. You chose your work for a reason. They chose you for a reason too. The reason is that the methodologies you've identified in your mission statement are also a part of your corporate community's means of reaching the community vision.

Let's take a quick look at why you're in the company you're in now, and what role that has already played in leading you towards your definition of a meaningful life. We're going to need your personal mission statement, and the mission statement (or similar) of your organization. If your company doesn't have one, that's ok, pick one from a company that you aspire to work with in the future. Trust me, it will help. Go ahead and write the company mission here:

_____

_____

_____

_____

Can you see how your organization's mission is contributing to achieving your vision from the last chapter? You want to achieve your vision for your life, and you chose this company through which you could accomplish that vision. Can you see how being with this economic community might help you do that? If you look through the behavioral lens of the mission, there should be a more or less understandable path to the vision. You should be able to say, "Yes, if we do these things outlined in the mission, we will move in the direction of our vision."

Do you remember AMG's vision statement?

AMG's vision
Growing Together, Delivering Value,
Embracing Heritage

Well, this is their mission statement:

AMG's mission
We commit to building profitable relationships with our business partners by investing in our community, employees and customers, in order to make them happy.

Can you see how the dominant methodology of building profitable relationships that make people happy is a recipe for growing together, delivering value, and embracing heritage?

Business is Personal

When I was in the room with the Executive Committee, helping them choose these meaningful words, I was really impressed by the tension that they created between the words *profitable* and *happy*.

Among AMG's group of companies is an automotive distributor. They sell Nissan, Renault, and Infiniti cars in Abu Dhabi. Now, it's easy to see how customers might be really happy if AMG just started giving away all of their cars. I'm pretty sure that would make me happy as a customer. But it's not profitable. And it's easy to see how withholding bonuses and raises, cutting salaries and staff, might build a profitable relationship for the company's business partners in the short-term, but it most certainly wouldn't make the employees happy.

The genius in these meaningful words is that happiness and profitability end up being two sides of the same coin. Unprofitable happiness is just as unfavorable of an outcome as profitable unhappiness. For the leaders at AMG, one cannot, and should not, exist without the other.

I recall that during those meetings we also had a long discussion about the word "happy." Should it be "happiness" instead? But it was decided that the word "happiness" had become a bit of a cliché, since the UAE has a Minister of Happiness, and most government offices there are called Happiness Centers now. Happiness metrics are ubiquitous in Human Resources these days, so a more unique and deliberate phrasing was chosen so that the final word in the mission would be "happy."

It was also mutually recognized that they didn't just want happiness for their stakeholders in a general sense, but rather to communicate through these meaningful words the intention of the organization to be an active contributor in making them happy. Passively achieved happiness is not sufficient to meet the demands of this mission. The corporate community is committed to help proactively foster happiness.

It's amazing to me how much thought and debate goes into such simple words and phrases during these strategy processes. Facilitating these community statements in a range of companies has not only been fulfilling to my own mission, it also happens to be an awesome privilege. That's not merely a coincidence.

I took more than a hundred senior staff in AMG through the leadership program that helped them build their personal vision, mission, values, and goals statements. Due to some confusion between vision and mission in the writings of a few popular management authors, mission was the most difficult concept on the strategy map for the AMG staff to understand and grasp. If you think you've got it, that's great. But I'll outline a few examples for you just in case.

Miriam sees herself as a person who 'welcomes and cares for everyone' as part of her personal mission. Welcoming and caring for everyone is Miriam's methodology for reaching her vision of caring for her family and helping her community. So, it isn't a surprise that she found her niche as a front desk clerk in the hospitality industry. Her mission is not only helping her achieve a high quality of care for her family and community, it also contributes to the hotel's mission of providing excellent hospitality for its guests.

Jeff is mechanically inclined and enjoys making things work, so it's totally natural that he works as a maintenance manager. His love for fixing things helped him find a parallel methodology for success with (and in) a furniture factory. The factory's mission included quality craftsmanship, which Jeff knew required the high-end machinery that he maintained. He found meaning in protecting the community's quality craftsmanship by maintaining the machines to the best of his ability.

James from AMG is a Property Manager. Do you remember James from Chapter 4? His vision is like this:

James' vision
Be an approachable and dynamic leader
and friend, constantly inspiring and
empowering those around me.

During the training, James had to write his mission statement. Here's how he described the methodology by which he would achieve being the dynamic, inspiring, and empowering leader, and friend he envisioned himself to be:

James' mission
To lead by example, interact more at
home and work. Further my career and

knowledge by seeking out opportunities that test my abilities so I can identify how to further improve mine and others, lives & professional goals whilst benefiting from the journey and rewards it offers.

Let's briefly break this down. James spends more than half his life in property management at AMG, and yet, I see no mention of property or management here whatsoever. Did James get it wrong?

Nope.

First of all, these words only need to be meaningful to James. But secondly, Property Manager is a role, not a dominant methodology. If it was a dominant methodology for James, it would be included here. Instead, his methodologies are:

1. Lead by example
2. Interact more at home
3. Interact more at work
4. Further career and knowledge
5. Seek out opportunities to test my abilities
6. Identify how to
   a. Improve my life & professional goals
   b. Improve the lives of others and their professional goals
7. Benefit from the journey
8. Benefit from the rewards of the journey

These are James' dominant methodologies: lead, interact, further, seek, identify, improve, benefit. And they will be exercised both in others' and his home and work lives. Now, can you see a clear path from exhibiting those kinds of behaviors to his ultimate vision of becoming "an approachable and dynamic leader and friend, constantly inspiring and empowering those around [him]"? I sure can. If James aligns his decisions to his mission, he is likely to succeed in his vision.

When I asked James to write it out for me, he clarified it like this:

James' mission	AMG's mission
interact more at home and work	= building profitable relationships
seeking out opportunities	= investing in our community
further improve mine and others' lives	= in order to make them happy

James saw direct parallels between the words he used to describe his own methodology in life and those of his corporate community. How cool is that? Now, you don't have to see what James sees here, but that doesn't matter — it only needs to be meaningful to James. James has half of his life wrapped up in this project.

What words or concepts can you see in your company's mission statement that resonate for you? You don't have to connect to all of it, but since it's governing about half of your life every day, it's unlikely that you will connect to none of it.

Your Mission	Your Company's Mission

1. What fresh meaning can you discover in comparing your mission to that of your company?
2. Can you see how you being part of this organization aligns with the organization's mission?

3. Can you see how you being part of this organization aligns with your own personal mission?

Remember, your job role isn't your whole life, but it is about half of it. So, you should be able to find meaning when you look through the lenses of both your own and your company's mission. What you do at work is a big part of who you are in general.

CHAPTER 6

Mutual Values: Who we are in community

My Values

It was a cold day in Ottawa, about -5 degrees Celsius (about 40 degrees Fahrenheit), but not cold enough to keep a couple of foolhardy brothers from killing a Saturday afternoon by exploring the banks of the Ottawa river. My younger brother Cris was always very supportive of my less-than-well thought-through plans for adventure. Even then, my mantra was, "pull the trigger, nudge the bullet," (act now, and steer during execution). Having said that, on this particular occasion, he looked more than a little skeptical when I announced my plan to cross the river from the Ontario side to the Quebec side — on an iceberg.

It seemed to me exactly the kind of thing a 13-year-old boy should attempt in winter. We rode our bikes down the street and past the park gate onto the path that flanked the river-bank. Then, seeing that the ice was thick along the shore, we stopped, rested our bikes on the ground, and walked down to the edge. I tentatively stepped onto the ice. It was strong enough to hold me, not by much, but enough to know I wouldn't sink if I stood still.

I looked across the river towards my destination. It looked about 600 meters (2000 feet) across. The current was fast, swollen with early spring runoff from the mountains. Waves could be seen bulging up from the middle of the river. It was dangerous. Very. Dangerous.

But it would be my moment of glory, and all I could see was the forbidden kingdom of Quebec taunting me to breach her shores like a conquering knight on a snow-covered steed.

From time to time, a small free-floating chunk of ice would drift past us, near enough for me to make a small run and jump onto it. But no run was needed, a larger piece of ice, about 4 meters wide, had just touched the shore a few meters away from us. This was my chance.

Holding my arms out for balance, I ran over and jumped onto the middle of the piece of ice, telling Cris to stay on shore and make sure the coast was clear, literally. I used a stick to push my craft away from the shoreline and just like that, I was sailing down a rushing river on a raft of ice.

The current picked me up and I started to drift towards the center of the river. I could see the rapids I would need to cross, and just beyond it, the great kingdom of Quebec, my prize. Cris ran along the shore now, struggling to keep up, looking more and more afraid as my speed picked up again. He was scared now, and yelling at me to come back. *Perhaps I should go back*, I thought, *Cris looks really worried. And I'm his big brother.*

"Just hang on, I'm coming back!" I yelled.

I was several meters from the shore now, and moving quickly. I tried to employ my stick as a paddle, but it was futile. I would have to trust the river, and the crossing would have to wait for another day. I waited for the ice to drift again towards the shoreline. And miraculously, as if in response to my very will, it did.

The ice crept, once again, towards the riverbank, and seeing that it probably wouldn't touch again, I decided that the only reasonable means of escape would be to jump. I backed up on the ice until the river started to flow up onto the back edge of it. And I crouched down, biding seconds until the time was right.

Then the gap closed to just over a meter. *I can make it*, I reasoned. I committed all of my power to that first step. There was only room on the ice for two steps before I leapt. Having failed to account for the ice shifting under my weight and movement, I had less momentum, and more distance to cover, than I'd planned for when I reached my last step. Unable to stop, I threw myself as far ahead as I could.

And I missed.

I landed splashing onto the shore, waist deep in freezing water, and scrambled out as quickly as I could. It was frigid. My whole body inhaled reflexively. My jeans quickly froze to my legs, and my winter boots were full of water. We were, by now, far from our bikes. As we made our way back up the river bank, I tried to look brave and not shiver.

Mom will kill me, I thought. I needed to be dry when I got home so that she wouldn't suspect the quest and prescribe some kind of punishment for my attempted border crossing. I climbed onto my bike, shaking, and hoped that riding as quickly as possible would somehow dry out my jeans before I reached home.

It didn't.

I don't remember what excuse I offered to my mother for being wet, but I do remember being very sick after that.

I made another attempt that summer, this time on a set of old wooden stairs that Cris and I found in the forest. Equally unsuccessful. I abandoned my campaign, conceding the land of Quebec to the river's defenses.

Yes, I could have died, but in those days, I was not governed by a fear of death. A higher order value was at play. I burned to know what was on the other side. I wondered if the journey could be undertaken, and if I would be the one to accomplish it.

Curiosity, and childhood bravado. Nothing more.

There were further curiosity-fueled junctures of ambition on the path ahead of me. When I was 23, I wondered if I could make an impact in the small post-Soviet nation of Estonia. At 26, I wondered if I could build a consulting career without working for any of the big consultancies. Two years later, I wondered if I could get into a masters' program without a bachelors' degree. By 30, I was wondering how it would be to raise our children in Yemen. At 34, I wondered what the Qur'an said to Christians and where Christians might have made errors interpreting it. At 36, I wondered if I could do an MBA and DBA back-to-back while being an entrepreneur at the same time. When I was 40, I wondered if Corporate Social Responsibility was an inevitable and evolutionary expression of community behavior among humans. When I was 41, I wondered if I could make a living as a solopreneur strategist. At 43, I wondered if I could run the Spartan Trifecta over a single weekend.

In contrast to my ill-fated river-crossing escapades, I succeeded in each of these attempts. With my curiosity satiated, I would move on to the next challenge. Today, I wonder if I can write a book on vision, mission, values, and goals, to help people connect with and find meaning in the half of their lives they spend at work, in less than one month.

How am I doing so far?

All of these adventures — hundreds of client companies, four post-graduate degrees, working in more than thirty countries — all of it, stems ultimately from my dominant core values.

> *My values*
> Curiosity. Generosity. Loyalty. Destiny.
> Passion.

The strongest of which is, by a freezing river's breadth, curiosity.

What Are Values?

If the vision is *why*, and the mission is *how* ... values answer the question of *who*. Who are you, really? What kind of person are you, and what kinds of decisions do you consistently make?

Values are underlying biases toward certain kinds of decisions. They lead to action. This is very important, because many people struggle with the distinction between spoken values and espoused values. A spoken value is something you say is important to you. An espoused value is something that comes out through your hands and feet, it is manifested by a constant stream of behavior that evinces the value and makes it visible to others, whether you recognize it or not.

If there's no evidence of it in your behavior, it's not a value, it's an intention. Intentions are only interesting to you. No one else in your life will ever see your intentions. Real values are espoused through consistent behavior that make them visible to others.

Simon Sinek suggests that we should write down our values as verbs, never nouns. My value of curiosity then might be rendered as: being curious. Or my value of generosity would be: being generous. He suggests that adjectives like honesty are not helpful because they are not actionable, so they should be replaced with actions such as: always tell the truth. Innovation, in Simon's view cannot be a value, since it is not possible to know what being more innovative looks like. It's therefore not actionable.[27]

I agree with Sinek that values must be actionable, but I do not agree with him that they need to be expressed as verbs. I also disagree that people don't know the behaviors associated with being innovative. I think Sinek is confusing the concepts of virtue and directive here. A virtue, like a value, is an adjective or noun given to a quality of something. A directive is the instruction given to support or produce that quality. Honesty is a virtue. "Always tell the truth" is a directive. Anyway, Sinek and I have travelled well on the personal strategy path until now. Here is where we part ways. But as always, the only important meaning is the one that's created in your head, so if expressing your values as verbs is helpful for you, go right ahead. Just don't feel trapped in it.

In *Beyond Talent*, leadership expert John Maxwell writes, "Core values give order and structure to an individual's inner

---

[27] Sinek, S. *Values are Verbs – 2019 [Video file]*. Retrieved December 22, 2019, from https://www.youtube.com/watch?v=o3Va_Y4cDSg

life, and when that inner life is in order, a person can navigate almost anything the world throws at him [or her]."[28] I like this definition since it pictures values as internal things that involuntarily generate external responses. When life throws something at a leader, they will respond with behaviors that reveal their true values.

One of my early mentors, John Caplin, once told me: "Behaviors don't determine our values, but reveal them." And this sits right with me, even now. You can't say you value honesty by telling yourself to always tell the truth, as Sinek suggests. You can only say that you value honesty if telling the truth is already an identifiable and dominant behavior pattern. So, when I invite you to write your values, my encouragement would not be to create adjectives to express values you wish you had, but creating adjectives to describe the values that you already espouse.

Aubrey Malphurs would probably agree with me. In his 1996 and 2004 editions of *Values-Driven Leadership*, Malphurs proposes values as the foundations upon which organizational vision is constructed. He proposes ten benefits to the articulation of values, both personally and organizationally, which I have paraphrased:

1. Values empower an individual/organization to clarify their/its distinctiveness.

---

[28] Maxwell, J. C. (2011). Beyond Talent: Become Someone Who Gets Extraordinary Results. *Thomas Nelson*.

2. Values help people outside of an organization determine if this organization is for them.
3. Values communicate what is important to the individual/organization.
4. Values help people embrace positive change. They determine what change will be helpful or harmful to the individual/organization.
5. Values influence overall behavior. They drive goals set, decisions made, problems solved, and so on.
6. Values inspire people to action.
7. Values enhance credible leadership.
8. Values clarify an individual's/organization's character. They affect how work is conducted.
9. Values contribute to success by generating deeper personal involvement.
10. Values determine an individual's/organization's vision. They are the hidden motivators that guide the selection of the vision.[29]

Most of this can be found in the writings of other strategists and practitioners, but the last one is truly remarkable. Malphurs suggests that values are the real root of the vision. What do you think? I think he's right. I think it's not possible to produce a vision for your life that doesn't embrace your core values. Think about it. How can you aim to achieve something if you don't already possess the values that drive

---
[29] Malphurs, A. (1996). *Values-driven Leadership: Discovering and Developing Your Core Values for Ministry*. *Grand Rapids, Michigan: Baker Books.*

the consistent behaviors leading you in that direction? You can't aim to be rich if you do not already value monetizing your work. If you're consistently doing things for people for free, then, probably, being rich isn't going to be in your vision.

No one is perfect, and no one behaves with total consistency in anything all of the time. Remember your humanity, and think of a value as a default orientation. At any moment, you can make a conscious decision to behave in opposition to your values. Values then could be described as the default decision-making orientations that lead to behaviors that contribute to accomplishing a vision.

I want to add something here. Values should be both descriptive and aspirational. They should both accurately describe your dominant decision-making and behavior in the past, and indicate a kind of quality that you would like to pursue in the future. In this sense, a value is both characteristic of you, and inspirational for you.

Way back in 2006, when I was writing my Personal Life Mandate, I identified several core values:

Holistic	Effective	Cultural	Quality
Lifestyle	Tools	Knowledge	Legacy
Integrity	Faith	Generosity	Rest
Mentoring	Intentional		

First of all, too many. That's a good start, but I did well to cut it down to five about a decade later. That made the list easier to remember, and gave me less to focus on. As a rule of thumb, use as few words as you can without leaving out something meaningful. You can always change them later, upon reflection.

Second ... integrity? Seriously. Who did I think I was?

Integrity originates from the Latin *integer*, which stands for a whole number, without any division or fraction. And integer is a negative form of *tangere* (to touch), rendering the meaning, untouched. Think about that for a minute. Integrity is the quality of being untouched, or perhaps in the case of a value, untouchable. Yikes!

I've heard it likened to sincerity which has an interesting etymology. In Dan Brown's, *The Lost Symbol*, as in popular discourse, sincere is said to have originated from the Latin *sine* (without) and *cera* (wax). It is said that in ancient Greco-Roman times, a sculptor would fill the cracks in pottery with wax, so that pieces could be sold for more money. A piece that was genuinely perfect had no cracks, and was therefore "without wax," *sine cera*. It's a nice story, but almost certainly untrue historically.

The proper etymology of sincerity is Latin, but derived from *sin* (one) and *crescere* (growth). It's meant to denote a harvest of only a single type of grain. *Crescere* is also the root word behind cereal. So, the meaning is still connected to the concept of purity and being made of only one thing, but not in the way that it's been commonly understood.

In any case, I scrapped integrity, not because I have none, but because its true meaning is akin to flawlessness and perfection, and I thought it disrespectful to God and negligent of my own flaws to claim it as a value. I am neither perfect, flawless, nor untouchable. Just ask my wife!

Integrity was scrapped, but the relational aspect of it was still important to me, so integrity and mentoring together became *loyalty*. *Curiosity* and *passion* were values I identified in subsequent inventories of my actual behaviors. Over the ensuing years, I also consolidated terms like *faith*, *intentional legacy*, and *holistic lifestyle* into a new word: *destiny*.

Looking at a brief history of my life, starting with the iceberg fiasco, I discovered how salient curiosity was for me, even though I hadn't recognized it in the first draft of my values. The risk-taking and road-less-travelled behaviors I mentioned above have been consistent for me, so my value of curiosity was discovered when I looked at my long history of consistent curiosity-driven behaviors. I mean seriously, who does a PhD solely because they're curious about something? Well, I do.

The same was true for passion, which came out of thoughtful reflection on real world behaviors such as my tolerance for risk and ambiguity, my preference to be working on several difficult challenges all at the same time, and the speed and depth to which I build meaningful relationships in my life. Passion comes from the Latin *passio*, meaning, "to suffer." It's not a warm and friendly term, but one intended to reflect the consistency with which I face, rather than shy away from, suffering. Biking home in frozen wet jeans in 1988 was as much a kind of opt-in for suffering as was living in Yemen in 2011. Like it or not, it's who I am.

What are the kinds of decisions that you consistently make?

What kind of person are you?

Your Values

I showed you mine, now it's your turn. I want you to think about the kind of person you are, and the kinds of decisions you make. If you were at an interview, not for a job, but for friendship, and you were asked to describe yourself in three or four words (or terms), what words would they be?

_____   _____

_____   _____

Would other people in your life describe you with the same words? Think of the people closest to you outside of work;

what words have they used, or would they use, to describe you? Write three or four down:

_____   _____

_____   _____

What about people outside of work? What about your partner or spouse? Your children? Your parents? Your neighbors or friends? What words have these people used, or would use, to describe the kind of person you are?

_____   _____

_____   _____

Let's do an integrity check here, just to see if there are any cracks in what you've just written down. We often don't see ourselves clearly, since we can judge ourselves by our intentions rather than our behaviors. We need other people to tell us that our behaviors line up (or not) with what we think our values are.

So, I want you to ask two people at work, and two people outside of work, to describe you in three words each. Yes, you will have to send them messages on WhatsApp or Messenger or whatever app you use. You can use this as an opener:

> "Hey there. I'm working on a personal project at the moment and I would really value your input on

something. If you had to describe me in only three words, what would they be?"

Person 1 _____ describes me as:

_____

Person 2 _____ describes me as:

_____

Person 3 _____ describes me as:

_____

Person 4 _____ describes me as:

_____

While you await their replies, I've got another brainstorming activity for you. I've actually prepared a list of nearly 400 value words that you can use to get your imagination going in this part. Go to Appendix A at the back of the book (page 193 onward) and follow the instructions there.

By now, you will have several lists going: words you would use to describe yourself, words you think others would use to describe you, words that others actually use to describe you, and words you circled on the list in Appendix A.

From all of these lists, can you isolate the words that stand out to you most? Remember, you're not describing your intentions here, you're describing the values that inform your actual behaviors, and the kinds of behaviors you would like to continue to exhibit in the future. Try to narrow the list down to 15 words or less. There's no wrong answer, so just be free. Write them here:

_____   _____

_____   _____

_____   _____

_____   _____

_____   _____

_____   _____

_____   _____

_____   _____

The next step is to see where your personal values and those of your corporate community overlap. Be gracious as you enter this section though. We tend to judge others more harshly than we judge ourselves, and we tend to judge our companies even harsher than other individuals.

Mutual Values

You're only human, so don't expect your behavior to align perfectly with your values. Your company is also made up of humans, so it's even more difficult to regulate. You'll have hundreds, maybe thousands of individuals all judging themselves by their intentions and each other by their behaviors. You can expect one or more corporate values to be broken regularly by the behaviors of any member of that organization. That doesn't mean the values are not values; it just means that it's tough to find consistent behavior across a number of humans for any extended period of time. We need to be more patient and forgiving if we're to live harmoniously in community.

Your behavior is governed by your values, and half of all your behaviors are exhibited at work. Therefore, we should expect that any person, who inhabits a corporate community for any length of time, should have some overlap between the behaviors they expect of themselves and the behaviors the community expects of its members. After all, you were chosen to be a member of that community not just because of your CV, but because you're the kind of person that would fit in. It's your values, who you are, that got you the job.

So, let's take a look at the kind of person that your organization was expecting when they hired you. What are the values of your organization?

_____   _____

_____   _____

_____   _____

_____   _____

You are only a member of the community, not the whole community, so if you don't personally connect with every value, that's totally fine. Do any of these words stand out to you as more meaningful than others? Circle them.

Let's look at another community. Do you remember AMG's vision and mission statements?

AMG's vision
Growing Together, Delivering Value,
Embracing Heritage

AMG's mission
We commit to building profitable relationships
with our business partners by investing in
our community, employees and customers,
in order to make them happy.

After our long discussion on values, you should be able to see, in the vision and mission statements, that in order to achieve this vision through the activities outlined in this mission, a certain kind of person will need to be on the team. So, let's see if the values of AMG line up with the rest of the strategy so far:

AMG's values
Excellent. Empowered. Engaged.
Optimistic. One Team.

Can you see how any individual that describes themselves as excellent, empowered, engaged and optimistic might fit into a team that is building happy and profitable relationships on a journey to grow together, deliver value, and embrace heritage? The value of *one team* is a direct triangulation of the vision elements of growing together and embracing heritage. And the value of being optimistic is a direct reflection of the mission element of making people happy. There are several more semantic connections here, but we'll leave it at that for now.

I remember, when AMG's staff and I were framing these values, there was a lengthy discussion about the form of the words themselves. We debated whether they should be adjectives (engaging or engaged), or nouns, (engagement). We didn't consider Sinek's option of using verbs/directives such as "be engaging," because verbs felt too forced, and lacking in optimism. The verb form, "be engaging," may carry the assumption that one is not yet engaged. But to say that someone is engaged, as an adjective in the past tense, assumes that they in fact already are. I suppose there are benefits and drawbacks either way, but in the end, what's important is that the words are meaningful to the members of the community, not to spectators like you and me, or Sinek.

The AMG executive leadership decided that the values should be words that complete the implicit sentence, "We are ..." which I thought was a wonderful choice. It requires optimism to say that a whole community is optimistic, engaged, and empowered. It speaks to the default orientation of hope among the leadership that wishes to communicate to its community that "We are not aspiring to be one team; we *are* one team. We are not trying to be engaging, and we don't just say we value engagement, we *are* engaged, right now."

I went through a sanity check with more than a hundred managers in the company and asked them all, "Is this true of us? Are we excellent, engaged, optimistic, and empowered? Are we all one team?" And the resounding response was YES. The management felt that though no one value was executed perfectly at any given time, the community's orientation toward those values produced cultural behaviors that evinced them far more often than not, and certainly enough to say that they had been culturally embedded. They *are* empowered. They *are* one team.

And when it was time for us to add James' values to his vision and mission as part of the process, I wasn't at all surprised by them.

James' vision
Be an approachable and dynamic leader and friend, constantly inspiring and empowering those around me.

James' mission
To lead by example, interact more at home and work. Further my career and knowledge by seeking out opportunities that test my abilities so I can identify how to further improve mine and others' lives & professional goals whilst benefiting from the journey and rewards it offers.

James' values
Approachable. Inspirational. Empowering. Interactive. Energetic. Curious.

The words approachable, inspiring, and empowering occur in both his values and his vision. It's a direct line from the kind of person he is to the kind of thing he wants said of him at his funeral. His value of being curious is reflected in his methodology of seeking knowledge. And being interactive is reflected in the thread of benefiting other people in both his vision and mission. Energetic is a property of the effort that he puts into all of these activities and value-driven behaviors.

When James got up to present his values, he paralleled them like this:

James' values	AMG's values
Approachable	= Engaged
Inspirational	= Excellent
Empowering	= Empowered
Interactive	= One team
Energetic & Curious	= Optimistic

James' connection between his energetic and curious values, and the corporate value of optimistic is interesting to me. I don't necessarily connect those concepts. But for James, the act of energetic curiosity *is* an act of optimism. He doesn't see them as dissociated at all. Pessimism would be reflected as lack of curiosity and lack of energy. I really liked his definition here.

There's no wrong definition. I have the greatest difficulty in convincing boards of directors to avoid the temptation of defining their values. Invariably, once corporate values are written down and agreed upon, someone in the room will insist that we define them, so that employees don't misinterpret them.

This is a trap. Once you have a meaningful set of value words, the least effective thing you can do with them is to define them. Every bit of definition that the leadership adds to the words restricts the ability of the employees to create meaningful connections with them in their own minds. The only definition that matters is the definition created in the employees' head when they read the words and take them to heart. That's all. If your intent is to govern behavior, use the Employee Handbook, but don't steal away meaning from corporate values.

Let's close this chapter with a look at your values and those of your corporate community.

Your Values	Your Company's Values

1. Can you draw direct parallels between any of your values and those of your company?
2. Are any of your values contributing factors in behaving according to the values of your organization?
3. Can you behave according to all of the values of your company without breaching any of your own values?
4. Is it becoming a little more clear why you chose to be in a community represented by these values?
5. What new meaning can you see from this for your life?

Remember, your job role isn't your whole life, but it is about half of it. So, you should be able to find meaning when you look through the lenses of both your values and your company's values. Who you are at work is at least half of who you are, so some blend and blur between your values and those of your corporate community is to be expected.

And now that we have a pretty good understanding of where you're going (vision), how you're getting there (mission), and what kinds of decisions you will make (values), it's time to identify milestones along the way. This is how you will remain focused, and measure your progress. We will be producing your personal goals, and discussing how achieving your company's goals will help you reach your own.

CHAPTER 7

Mutual Goals: What we are accomplishing together

My Goals

It was the morning of November 14, 2019. I looked out the window just to be sure I knew where I was and that I was ok with what was about to happen. The weather was perfect, my heart was clean, and my focus, unwavering. I was prepared to fail in a significant goal.

A year prior, in December 2018, I had run all three Spartan obstacle course races in two days, and had made it a goal of mine to do the same this year. I remember running the 23 km (14.2 mile) Beast on Friday morning. Running miles over mountains, through soft sand, carrying buckets of rocks and climbing over walls to complete the ordeal. I remember fatigue setting in, and having to will my way through the last few miles of the race. It was grueling. At the end, I dragged myself to meet my then girlfriend, Nicole, at the hotel. She said I looked like my ghost. I was wasted from the inside out, and bleeding in several places.

The following morning, I dropped my leg over to the side of the bed and let it fall to the floor. It was 5 am, and time to get ready for the 13 km (8 mile) Super race. I was hoping my heel would have stopped bleeding overnight, but it hadn't. It was raw and wet. I picked up my shoes to inspect the damage again. The back of my shoe was torn and completely open, exposing a piece of plastic meant to offer support, the edge of which had shred my heel the day before.

I didn't have spares.

I forced my bleeding foot into the torn shoe once again, and made my way to the starting line. The next race would start soon. The crowd was cheering, and I was desperately struggling to shove a piece of cardboard into my heel to create some padding between the skin and plastic. And then the bullhorn cried out, "Spartans! What is your profession?" To which the crowd replied, "Aroo! Aroo! Aroo!"

But not me. I didn't reply. I stood in silent protest against the torment I had orchestrated for myself. It was a goal I had set, and it would need to be achieved, by me, or not at all. All three races. Which meant, even after I ran the next 13 km (8 mile) race, a 7 km (4.5 mile) sprint was further awaiting me, and I would have to both start, and finish, that race as well.

The first steps across the starting line were the hardest. After that, I broke the race down into 100 strides at a time, and willed myself to keep going. And going. And going.

Mutual Goals: What we are accomplishing together

By day's end, I had earned my way to the finish line for the third time. I scaled the wall, jumped over fire, collected my medal, and collapsed on the grass. Nicole brought me water, told me she loved me and was proud of me. "One day," I thought, "I'm going to marry her." I was proud of myself as well. I had set up a goal with a reasonable chance of failure, and I had succeeded.

A month later, I set my goals for 2019. At the top of the list was to run the three-race Spartan Trifecta again, in a single weekend. I held onto that goal throughout the year, and waited hungrily for the dates to be announced. It would be November 15-16, 2019.

The anticipated weekend had finally come, but I wasn't even there. I stared out the window on this perfect day, and just for a moment, I thought about the cost of getting to this place in my life for a second time, ready to face this challenge once again. I imagined the racers far away, lacing up their shoes this morning, fueling up with oats, and getting themselves ready for the Beast once again. I cheered them on in my heart. Then, I let go of my Spartan Trifecta goal for 2019 and turned away from the window, and away from the race, to face Nicole.

My goal of completing the Spartan Trifecta was more than 11,000 kms (6,800 miles) away in Oman.

And today was our wedding day in Australia.

A few hours later, I stood between a row of trees in Fitzroy Gardens, Melbourne. The grass and trees were spring green, and Joey was standing beside me. He has been my best friend since high school, and was reprising his role as the Best Man at my wedding. We were joined by Joey's wife, Lindsay, and Nicole's best friend, Vesna. And that was it, the whole wedding party was there.

It is quite a different thing to get married compared to running three Spartan races over a weekend; yet, no less effortful, and certainly much more rewarding.

Nicole looked spectacular in her white dress, carrying a simple bouquet of flowers. We struggled to say our vows without breaking into tears. After the ceremony, Joey turned to me and said, "Congratulations. I'm proud of you, man." I was proud of myself as well. I had set a goal with a reasonable chance of failure, and I had succeeded.

I didn't give the Spartan Trifecta another thought. That is, until New Year's Day the following year when I counted the goal as a happy failure in favor of a higher goal. Then I wrote it down again for the next year. Spartan Trifecta in two days.

My goals for 2019 were to:

1. Publish a book.
2. Take my kids on a one-week international vacation.
3. Run 6 Obstacle Course Races (OCRs).

4. Run the Spartan Trifecta in two days.
5. Achieve a press-to-handstand.
6. Read not less than two books per month.
7. Deliver not less than four keynote speeches.
8. Complete my Artificial Intelligence education at M.I.T.
9. Work in the UAE public sector as a consultant.
10. Successfully relocate my 18-year-old son Gabriel to Canada.
11. Finish my tattoo project.
12. Propose to, and marry, the last love of my life.

I did not accomplish them all, as you are now aware. Here are the ones I failed to achieve:

1. I finished writing, but didn't publish my book before the end of the year. I missed the goal timeline, but completed the core achievement.
4. You know about this one. It just so happened that the year I married my second wife, Nicole, the Spartan Trifecta weekend was announced to be held on our wedding day. I had to choose between one goal or the other. But the choice was easy. I had priorities, and one was much more long-term and life-affirming.
5. I found out this year that I have a blood pressure issue that prevents me from doing inverted poses in yoga, and hand-stand pushups in CrossFit. No more inversions for me, so no press-to-handstand. I failed due to medical reasons. The price of getting older, I suppose.

What are Goals?

If vision is *why*, mission is *how*, and values are *who*, then goal-setting answers the "what and when" questions. What are you doing, exactly? And by when? A goal is an intention to complete a certain activity by a certain time. No doubt you have some experience in goal-setting. You've likely intended for something to happen in the future that would require some kind of commitment and effort on your part, and you've achieved it.

Why mess with quality, right? The best and most well-known structure for defining a goal is still the S.M.A.R.T. structure developed by George T. Doran in 1981.[30] As a reminder for those who know, and as an introduction for those who don't, Doran proposed that goals be defined as having five specific qualities.

Goals are:

> **S**pecific: they target a specific area for improvement.
> **M**easurable: they quantify, or at least suggest, an indicator of progress.
> **A**ssignable: they specify who will do it.
> **R**ealistic: they state what results can realistically be achieved given available resources.
> **T**ime-related: they specify when the result can be achieved.

---

30 Doran, G. T. (1981). *There's a S.M.A.R.T. Way to Write Management's Goals and Objectives.* Management Review, 70*(11)*.

I like this approach, though like many others, I have scrapped Doran's "Assignable" in favor of "Attainable" and Realistic in favor of "Relevant." Attainable means that the goal is potentially achievable, that it is within the realm of possibility that you will achieve it. It is interesting to have a goal to go to the moon, but since there's no commercial spaceflight planned yet, and unless you are in the astronaut training program, this is not a realistically attainable goal.

Relevant means that the goal is somehow related to your vision and mission. You might have a goal to eat 74 hot dogs in 10 minutes, and though it is measurable and time-related, unless you are a competitive eater, it's not relevant. Joey Chestnut is a competitive eater, and did, in fact, eat 74 hotdogs in 10 minutes in 2018. Good job for good job, Joey!

Lots of people have played with the S.M.A.R.T acronym. I've heard of the "R" being used to also denote Result-based, Resourced, Resonant, Realistic, and Reasonable. Over the years, some have also added an "er" to the end, rendering S.M.A.R.T.E.R.

> **E**valuated: appraisal of a goal to assess the extent to which it has been achieved.
> **R**eviewed: reflection and adjustment of your approach or behavior to reach a goal.[31]

---

31 Haughey, D. (2014). *A Brief History of SMART Goals*. Retrieved January 2, 2020, from https://www.projectsmart.co.uk/brief-history-of-smart-goals.php.

I don't add these in my personal use of the acronym. I think evaluation and review are redundant, but if you like them, be my guest. I also don't want too much rear-facing in the goal-setting process, and these are both past-oriented. They are pretty popular though. Your call.

For Sinek, goals might be called the "What" of his Golden Circle. He also suggests that goals should be unrealistic, because he believes that achieving a realistic or any finite goal can lead to depression. He cites Michael Phelps, who, after becoming the most awarded Olympic medalist in history, fell into depression. Why? Because his goals were finite, and when he had achieved them, his life felt bereft of purpose and meaning. He failed to make the transition from a finite game to an infinite game. Therefore, Sinek suggests that goals should be unrealistic, and infinite in nature.[32]

I agree with Sinek that achieved goals can lead to post-achievement depression. In this case, the last milestone in a great achievement is rewarded in the brain by a hit of dopamine, but when the whole series of milestones connected with the big goal are completed, the brain loses a powerful ongoing source of dopamine, and may slip into withdrawal. I disagree with Sinek that the way to tackle this is to have unrealistic or unachievably high goals, thereby ensuring that although you get dopamine hits from your progress, you never get bitten by the last-hit blues.

---

32 Sinek, S. *Simon Sinek Goals – 2018 [Video file]. (2018). Retrieved December 20, 2019, from https://www.youtube.com/watch?v=m29q4Yh4U_0*

Instead, I suggest having reoccurring and leapfrogging goals in multiple streams of achievement. I have a recurring goal to run a certain number of obstacle course races each year, and to read a certain number of books each month. Those are both reoccurring goals in different streams. For you, for example, career might be one stream, and family, another. You may achieve your graduation goal in an education stream, but that won't lead to depression if you have a concurrent writing goal in your career stream that isn't yet achieved. Always having something to work on is the key. And just as diversifying one's portfolio is good advice for the investor, it is also wise to avoid placing too many of your emotional eggs in any single goal basket.

That said, if you want to include a few infinite aims among your goals, please do so. If that helps motivate you, then it's valuable. But don't allow infinite goals to replace finite goal-setting. This is a trap that will likely lead you to justify your apathy or abandon the quest for an unreachable target.

But don't overcompensate by making your goals too easy. It can't be counted as a goal if it's immanent. If something is extremely likely to happen with minimal change in your level of effort, then it's not worth citing as a goal. For example, don't set a goal of "have a baby by the end of the year" if you're already pregnant. And don't write down your graduation as a goal if you are in your final year with a 3.5 GPA. These are too easy, too likely. Make your goals challenging and effortful but not unattainable.

Also, it's not helpful to write a goal over which you do not have control. I fell into that trap in 2019. In addition to the goals above, I wrote down a goal to meet H.H. Sheikh Mohammed bin Rashid Al Maktoum (the Ruler of Dubai) by the end of 2019. I really just wanted to meet him. He seems like a high-quality leader to me, and I thought I'd like to thank him for developing a great city in which to raise my kids. But it wasn't in my hands. I can't control, or even exert influence on the Sheikh's schedule. That was silly. So, I abandoned the goal half way through the year. Maybe I'll meet him one day, but that's a hope now, not a goal.

I would also like to meet Henry Mintzberg. He is my all-time favorite organizational strategist on the planet. He also cautions us to remember that while goals are as good as intentions, they should not be written in stone. Sometimes, our intentions crash into an iceberg of life and sink. A changing reality can have a significant impact on our ability to reach our goals, and even on the wisdom of keeping them. So, our intentions bend to accommodate reality, and this impacts our goals, both as individuals and as organizations. It's a concept Mintzberg calls emerging strategy.[33] I had a couple of significant life changes in 2018 that caused me to abandon my goal of completing my third doctorate that year. It was a good strategy choice.

---

33 Mintzberg, H. (1994). Rise and Fall of Strategic Planning. *Simon & Schuster.*

When I got to 2020, I had a new set of goals. Looking back, these lessons on goal setting took me a while to learn as well. The oldest list of my personal goals is from January 2010:

1. To complete a PhD in Arab and Islamic Studies by 2013.
2. To work for five different Yemeni companies by June 2010.
3. To publish a written work every five years from the age of 25 until death.
4. To put my children through the university program of their choice.
5. To receive my European day-rate for consulting services in the Middle East by 2013.
6. To acquire working knowledge of Arabic by the end of 2010.
7. To acquire academic proficiency in Arabic by the end of 2013.
8. To facilitate my wife into her ideal life-giving social role in Yemen.
9. To take my family for an international vacation for at least one week per year.
10. To read not less than one book every week.

I failed across the board. Haha. Goals #1, #2, #5, #9 and #10 are the only truly S.M.A.R.T and finite goals on the list. Goal #3 is an infinite recurring goal, whose pace, by the way, I'm crushing. In recent years, I have changed this from infinite wording to finite wording and recurring annually. It now reads "To publish a book" and I renew the goal every year, to require the writing of a new book.

Goal #4 was out of my hands. It was a good intention, but there were a lot of variables here, and I had made an assumption on my children's behalf that they would even want to go to university. That's not fair, so I scrapped that goal.

Goals #6 and #7 had to do with Arabic language acquisition, but they were not S.M.A.R.T. Can you pick out what was missing? Yup. Neither of these goals are measurable because I neglected to include the criteria. Who's to say what "working knowledge" or "academic proficiency" mean? It's too subjective. Instead, I completed a two-year Arabic program with honors. That was a much better goal.

Goal #8 was not S.M.A.R.T at all. It was out of my hands, completely subjective, and not time-bound. It was intended to communicate my commitment to seeing my wife in a positive social role in our new resident country, but it wasn't S.M.A.R.T, so it wasn't a goal. It was an intention. A good intention, and nothing more.

I'm glad I got better at this. If you look at my 2019 goals above, all of them are S.M.A.R.T. And so, my goal-setting became much more fruitful. I know what I want to accomplish in life, and I set up milestones each year to know that I am making progress. My vision and mission provide the destination and the mode of transport, my values govern the kinds of decisions I will make and behaviors I will exhibit. And my goals describe the pitstops and border crossings along the way.

I find strategic goal-setting more than a year in advance to be a bit restrictive. I like to remain flexible and responsive to the world around me. I add, remove, and alter goals throughout the year to ensure they are challenging yet achievable, and I review them every year. Occasionally, I'll have a longer term 3-/ 5-year goal. But I know other leaders that have clearly articulated 5- and 10- year goals. It's entirely up to you.

Your Goals

It's time to write a few goals of your own. I want you to concentrate first on writing S.M.A.R.T goals. Don't get sidetracked by writing infinite or reoccurring goals, those you can do later. Let's just work on a foundation that makes it clear that you are moving in the direction of your vision and mission.

Start by pulling the domains or arenas of success from your vision statement. What are the arenas in which you define success for yourself? Career, family relationships, education? Write each of them down here:

_____   _____

_____   _____

_____   _____

Now look at your mission statement and identify the individual domains and methodologies you will need to continuously develop to reach your vision. What are your preferred methodologies for reaching your vision? Reading and writing? Singing? Construction? Surgical practice? Public speaking? Write them down here:

_____   _____

_____   _____

_____   _____

_____   _____

If you are struggling with identifying areas of your life for which to record personal goals, please use the list below. You can (and should) have goals for yourself in each of these eight arenas of life.

1. Physical
2. Spiritual
3. Work or career
4. Family
5. Social relationships
6. Financial security
7. Mental improvement and attention
8. Fun

And don't forget, each goal needs to be S.M.A.R.T. We'll use my amended version of S.M.A.R.T for this.

> **S**pecific: target a specific area for improvement;
> **M**easurable: quantify, or at least suggest, an indicator of progress;
> **A**ttainable: it should be within the realm of possibility;
> **R**elevant: the goal should relate to your mission and vision somehow;
> **T**ime-related: specify when the results can be measured.

The wording of goals is also important. (Words are meaningful, remember?) We want the wording to be powerful, intentional, and motivating for you. We're answering the questions of what and when, so it should be in the following language:

I will *what* by *when*.

Let's take, for example, a goal in spiritual development. Some examples I've seen are:

- I will complete the Hajj before September 1, 2023.
- I will meditate for an average of 15 minutes, 5 days/week, for the whole year.
- I will read the entire Bible in a year.

Or perhaps, you don't have enough fun in your life, so a fun goal could look like this:

- I will visit two theme parks this year, and ride not less than six rollercoasters that I would consider scary.
- I will play snooker with my friends not less than two times each month. My father-in-law loves snooker; I've included this example as a nod to him.
- I will go out dancing not less than once every three months.

Each of those goals is specific, measurable, attainable, and time-bound, and depending on your personal mission and vision, they may also be relevant (related directly to your vision and mission). It's your turn now. You can use the domains you identified from your vision and mission above, and add one or two from the list of eight domains that I provided, and create your own goals. I'll give you room here to write down your first five.

Remember: I will *what* by *when*.

Goal #1. Domain: _____

I will _____

_____

Goal #2: Domain: _____

I will _____

_____

Mutual Goals: What we are accomplishing together

Goal #3. Domain: _____

I will _____

_____

Goal #4. Domain: _____

I will _____

_____

Goal #5. Domain: _____

I will _____

_____

Great work. Don't stop there though. You should write down as many goals as you would like to pursue to make a difference in all important areas of your life.

Mutual Goals

We tend to think of our personal goals and our corporate goals as mutually exclusive. Again, that's a bad hangover from terrible consulting in the 1970s and 1980s and doesn't belong here. As humans in economic communities, we rise together and fall together. We are all, every one of us, participating in economic communities for our own personal goals, but our ability to achieve them is equally bound in our ability to work together towards common goals.

If you complete your personal goals, do you think you will become a more powerful resource to your economic community? For example, let's say you have a goal to get in shape by losing 10 kgs (22 lbs) within the next four months. Do you think your weight loss will influence your performance at work? Absolutely. You will have more energy, more confidence, you will be more positive, sleep better, and make higher quality decisions because you are almost certainly eating healthier.[34]

If you have a goal to spend more time with your family, do you think you will be better at work? Definitely. You will be using your time more intentionally. You will spend less of your time at work feeling guilty and distracted about ignoring your family, and less time compensating for not spending time with them by using WhatsApp or Messenger at work. When your body is at work, your mind will be there too, because you have a clear goal for family time that you are protecting intentionally.

If you have a personal goal that is set by your work, it's usually called a Key Performance Indicator (KPI). It might

---

[34] Block, C. (2020). Chief Spartan Officer. *UAE: Passionpreneur Publishing.*

be a sales target or a project delivery date, but most of our jobs come with personal goals attached. Remember, your job is not all of you, but it's also not other than you. Your job KPIs *are* included in your personal goals.

That's the community's way of making sure each of its members are contributing profitably to their community relationship. And do you think that your achievement of KPIs contributes to your personal mission and vision as well? Of course. You are more likely to get a bonus, or a raise, or a promotion, if you are achieving your corporate goals. You are more likely to perform well if your KPIs are set high, too. And each KPI contributes to departmental and organizational KPIs, and those community KPIs are how the community determines whether it is succeeding or failing. If it is succeeding, all of its members benefit from secure sources of income, a stable working environment, and hopefully, if we're doing really well, a bonus at the end of the year.

What are the goals you've been asked to achieve at work? Write up to three of them here:

Goal #1. Domain: _____

I will _____

_____

Goal #2: Domain: _____

I will _____

_____

Goal #3. Domain: _____

I will _____

_____

Are your corporate goals also S.M.A.R.T? If not, can you reword them to make them S.M.A.R.T? Once they're S.M.A.R.T, they'll be easier for you to pursue because they'll be clearer.

Do you remember AMG's vision, mission, and values?

AMG's vision
Growing Together, Delivering Value,
Embracing Heritage

AMG's mission
We commit to building profitable relationships with our business partners by investing in our community, employees and customers, in order to make them happy.

AMG's values
Excellent. Empowered. Engaged.
Optimistic. One Team.

Mutual Goals: What we are accomplishing together

I can't share the company's corporate goals with you for contractual reasons. But I can share with you a few of the KPIs for James' role at AMG, taken directly from his own performance review document.

1. Promote diversity and inclusion through hiring goals (new recruits/year).
2. Identify efficiencies to Group entities to reduce operational costs by improving how space is occupied. Identify and engage cross-fertilization of services to optimize manpower and raise staff productivity.
3. Target reductions to Portfolio voids by X% from previous year. Identify and reduce operational costs throughout the year while maintaining asset integrity.
4. Identify and improve client perception of service levels through a specific questionnaire and feedback.
5. Deploy the 360 Feedback Score (Individual Survey Mean/Mean Survey Score) X Weight
6. Maintain and seek improvements to current policies, procedures and integration to ISO9001 requirements, along with employee performance and appraisals and KPI system.
7. Develop individuals to create and pursue career paths with staged and quantifiable targets as part of a diverse training program.

Strictly speaking, these are not S.M.A.R.T because I can't share the exact metrics and deadlines with you, but the point of the exercise is to see where James' work goals might interact with his personal strategy. Do you think there's a link between James' KPIs at work, and his corporate community's vision, mission and values? Absolutely! The whole point of a KPI is to focus individual efforts on corporate goals, which flow from the corporate vision, mission, and values.

Now, let's look at James' personal strategy:

James' vision
To be an approachable and dynamic leader and friend, constantly inspiring and empowering those around me.

James' mission
To lead by example, interact more at home and work. Further my career and knowledge by seeking out opportunities that test my abilities so I can identify how to further improve mine and others' lives & professional goals whilst benefiting from the journey and rewards it offers.

James' values
Approachable. Inspirational. Empowering. Interactive. Energetic. Curious.

James' goals
1. Lose 8kgs by March 31
2. Read a book every month
3. Reduce vacancies at work to 10% by end of year

4. Set aside 20 mins for strategy every week
5. Secure 4 new sponsors for a strategic marketing event
6. Enter 1 physical challenge every year
7. Restructure my department

Do you see any link between James' KPIs at work, and his personal vision, mission and values? Here are two that I see immediately:

1. James' vision of being "constantly inspiring and empowering" is supported by KPI nos. 1, 4, and 6.
2. James' mission to "identify how to further improve mine and others' lives & professional goals" is supported by KPI nos. 5 and 7.

James' personal goals #3, #4, #5 and #7 are also clearly related to his work. Those are goals that he set for himself, on top of his KPIs, so that he could measure his own efficacy as a community member of AMG. Can you see how securing four new sponsors for an event might contribute to the AMG mission of building profitable relationships with its business partners? Or what about James' goal of losing 8 kgs (18 lbs)? Will that have an influence on his happiness as an employee at AMG? Most certainly.

And can you see how not only would his goals boost the success of his economic community, but also facilitate achieving his personal vision and mission as well? Do you think that setting aside 20 minutes for strategy each week will contribute to James' vision of being a dynamic leader? You bet it will. And do you think if James reads a book every month it might help him further his career and knowledge? Absolutely!

James' goals are well aligned with both his personal vision and mission, and with those of his economic community. James is living a well-aligned life. He is living holistically, with a great work-life blend to keep him energized and interactive. There is no hard line between James' work life and his homelife. James isn't living two lives; he's living one life. One single blended life informed by and aligned to the meaningful words of his vision, mission, values and goals as a contributing member of a community with clear vision, mission, values and goals. What a blessing that is!

Your Turn

It's your turn now. Write down your corporate community's vision and mission, and see if you can connect your goals from above to any of the concepts in those statements.

Your Company's Vision:

_____

_____

Mutual Goals: What we are accomplishing together

_____

_____

Your Company's Mission:

_____

_____

_____

_____

Goal #_____ contributes to this word or phrase in my community's vision or mission:

_____

And it does so because:

_____

_____

Goal #_____ contributes to this word or phrase in my community's vision or mission:

_____

And it does so because:

_____

_____

Goal #_____ contributes to this word or phrase in my community's vision or mission:

_____

And it does so because:

_____

_____

1. Can you draw direct parallels between any of your goals and the vision or mission of your company?
2. Are any of your goals contributing factors in achieving career advancement in your current organization?
3. Can you pursue all of the KPIs set out for you in your company without breaching any of your personal values or betraying your personal vision and mission?
4. What new meaning can you see from this for your life?

If you are pursuing education on the side while working full-time, you will be able to apply your learning and your improved time management skills immediately to your job. You'll perform better at work as a result.

If your goals include physical exercise, it will improve your quality of thought, energy levels, and overall performance, both in and out of work.

If you are starting a side business, the skills you are learning in your personal business will be more easily applied as a best practice in your communications, negotiations, and sales efforts at work.

The fact is, none of us should be living dual lives. We are all unique and valuable individuals that have learned to value working together to build economic communities. Humans are wonderful and powerful social creatures. We need each other. And the better we are at finding alignment between our individual and communal roles, the more holistically, healthily, and happily we will live together.

Conclusion

Why am I *here*? And more importantly, why am *I* here?

We're almost done. I know it's been a lot of work, and I'm grateful that you've remained strong with me on this journey towards a more meaningful life at work.

If finding meaning at work was as simple as finding your passion, and getting people to pay you to do it, I would probably have people paying me to run obstacle course races, eat pizza, read books, and watch movies. But those activities don't add value to peoples' lives the way that a meaningful social role can. Strategy consulting, executive coaching, public speaking, and writing are all hard work, but they add value to my community and help me feed my family and educate my kids. Finding one's passion isn't necessarily about doing something different with your life; rather, it's about discovering and connecting passionately with what you are already doing with your life. I trust you have found some tools for that in the preceding chapters.

When you meet someone for the first time and they ask you your name and where you work, you'll hear it in a different light now. You'll know that they are trying to define you, because subconsciously they know that you are what you do. You are what you do not only in the little behaviors that make you unique to others, but in your job title, which indicates your social role to people trying to understand how to connect with you.

So, stop trying to balance your work and your life, and just embrace the truth that work is a big part of your holistic life. You are your work. It's not all of you, but it's not other than you either. It's about half of you, so you should make every effort to embrace your work-life blend, and recognize the meaningfulness of all the roles you play in society all at the same time, your work role included.

The words you use to describe yourself are powerful enough to subconsciously influence the decisions you make. And the words that organizations use to organize themselves are an opportunity to find meaning for a community of humans collaborating in an economic project. Your newly-articulated vision, mission, values, and goals are a powerful set of subconscious tools, not only to help drive your decision-making more intentionally, but to find meaning in the economic communities you partner with along the way.

Your vision is a description of the kind of future you would like to live in if everything goes well for you. It is why you exist, an outline of your life purpose. Your mission is a description of the dominant methodologies for reaching your vision. It is how you will make progress.

Your values describe who you are and the kinds of decisions you make. They are the foundation of your behaviors. And goals clearly describe what you are doing along the way. Goals describe milestones and progress steps so you can know you are always intentionally moving forward in all of the important areas of your life.

It's now time to answer the two most important questions concerning your current job:

> Why am I *here* (and not somewhere else)?
> Why am *I* here (and not someone else)?

Question 1: Why am I *here* and not somewhere else?

Well, for starters, you're human. As a survival instinct and to lead meaningful lives, we seek out communities in which we can play a valuable social role, so that together, our communities can compete with one another for resources on the planet in an elegant economic social game. You're here because teaming up with other humans is an evolutionary imperative.

Also, you're in your job as a result of every decision you've ever made. And since you're not a slave, or an idiot, you're here because you believe fundamentally that being in your current role is the best, fastest, most effective route to achieving your personal goals and reaching your life vision. If there was a better way available to you, you'd be doing that instead.

With those truths in mind, I want you to highlight three meaningful connections between your personal life strategy

Business is Personal

and the corporate strategy for your economic community. What three discoveries about your involvement in this community best describe why you've chosen to be in your current role at this time in your life?

I chose my current role in this specific community because:

One,

_____

_____

_____

Two,

_____

_____

_____

Three,

_____

_____

_____

Question 2: Why am *I* here and not someone else?

Your corporate community chose you for your role. You're there because your community believes you are the best person for that job at this time. Keep in mind that there are probably thousands of people on the planet that have your education and experience credentials. Your CV doesn't make you special ... your unique character does.

You were chosen because you are a "good fit" for the organization, both because your personal vision and mission are contributors to the overall vision and mission of the community, and because you are a certain kind of person. What kind of person are you for you to be chosen by a human community to do your particular job at this time, in this particular community?

I was chosen for my current role in this specific community because:

One,

_____

_____

_____

Two,

_____

Three,

And there it is.

Humans are remarkably talented at creating meaning for themselves. Has your job changed? Not really. But what about your view of yourself in your job. Has that changed? I sure hope it has improved a bit. Every bit of meaning in life counts.

Of course, words are not enough to create all of the meaning you are looking for at work. Healthy relationships are also a big part of finding and maintaining that sense of purpose and significance in your work. But as we approach the end of this book, I want to return to the imperative of building meaningful relationships at work.

And now, I need you to help me out a bit. I have two small favors to ask of you.

Conclusion: Why am I here? And more importantly, why am I here?

1. If you don't mind sharing, I'd love to hear your vision, mission, values, and goals, or as much of them as you are willing to send me. I'm collecting them, and I plan to use them to help others build more meaning into their lives in the future.
2. Please let me know what questions you still have. I am always looking to improve my quality of service to the world, and your feedback and unanswered questions will help me help others. I'll do my best to reply to you in person if you give me your email address. Good questions are almost always more fun for me than good answers.

Please take a minute and send those to me at: www.drcorrieblock.com/businessispersonal

It's been my absolute pleasure to share these insights with you. I hope these ideas are practical enough to be of use to you in any organization you choose to contribute a part of your meaningful life to.

I'm cheering for you!

Appendix A

Values List

This is not an exhaustive list, but I consider it exemplary. I've compiled these words over the last 20 years, and you are welcome to add to or disregard any of them. They are meant as a baseline for developing your own values. At first, only pay attention to the words you feel strongly about. If you are strongly drawn to a word, circle it, and if you strongly reject a word, strike it out. This will help you shorten the list and bring it into focus. After you've gone through it, review your circled words and put a star next to the top five. That will be your shortlist. Good luck.

Abundance
Acceptance
Accessibility
Accomplishment
Accuracy
Achievement
Acknowledgement
Activeness
Adaptability
Adoration
Adroitness
Adventure

Affection
Affluence
Aggressiveness
Agility
Alertness
Altruism
Ambition
Amusement
Anticipation
Appreciation
Approachability
Articulacy

Assertiveness
Assurance
Attentiveness
Attractiveness
Audacity
Availability
Awareness
Awe
Balance
Beauty
Being the best
Belonging
Benevolence
Bliss
Boldness
Bravery
Brilliance
Buoyancy
Calmness
Camaraderie
Candor
Capability
Care
Carefulness
Celebrity
Certainty
Challenge
Charity
Charm
Chastity

Cheerfulness
Clarity
Cleanliness
Cleverness
Closeness
Comfort
Commitment
Compassion
Completion
Composure
Concentration
Confidence
Conformity
Congruency
Connection
Consciousness
Consistency
Contentment
Continuity
Contribution
Control
Conviction
Conviviality
Coolness
Cooperation
Cordiality
Correctness
Courage
Courtesy
Craftiness

Appendix A: Values List

Creativity
Credibility
Cunning
Curiosity
Daring
Decisiveness
Decorum
Deference
Delight
Dependability
Depth
Desire
Determination
Devotion
Devoutness
Dexterity
Dignity
Diligence
Direction
Directness
Discipline
Discovery
Discretion
Diversity
Dominance
Dreaming
Drive
Duty
Dynamism
Eagerness

Economy
Ecstasy
Education
Effectiveness
Efficiency
Elation
Elegance
Empathy
Encouragement
Endurance
Energy
Enjoyment
Entertainment
Enthusiasm
Excellence
Excitement
Exhilaration
Expectancy
Expediency
Experience
Expertise
Exploration
Expressiveness
Extravagance
Extroversion
Exuberance
Fairness
Faith
Fame
Family

- Fascination
- Fashion
- Fearlessness
- Ferocity
- Fidelity
- Fierceness
- Financial independence
- Firmness
- Fitness
- Flexibility
- Flow
- Fluency
- Focus
- Fortitude
- Frankness
- Freedom
- Friendliness
- Frugality
- Fun
- Gallantry
- Generosity
- Gentility
- Giving
- Grace
- Gratitude
- Gregariousness
- Growth
- Guidance
- Happiness
- Harmony
- Health
- Heart
- Helpfulness
- Heroism
- Holiness
- Honesty
- Honor
- Hopefulness
- Hospitality
- Humility
- Humor
- Hygiene
- Imagination
- Impact
- Impartiality
- Independence
- Industry
- Ingenuity
- Inquisitiveness
- Insightfulness
- Inspiration
- Integrity
- Intelligence
- Intensity
- Intimacy
- Intrepidness
- Introversion
- Intuition
- Intuitiveness
- Inventiveness

Appendix A: Values List

- Investing
- Joy
- Judiciousness
- Justice
- Keenness
- Kindness
- Knowledge
- Leadership
- Learning
- Liberation
- Liberty
- Liveliness
- Logic
- Longevity
- Love
- Loyalty
- Majesty
- Making a difference
- Mastery
- Maturity
- Meekness
- Mellowness
- Meticulousness
- Mindfulness
- Modesty
- Motivation
- Mysteriousness
- Neatness
- Nerve
- Obedience

- Open-mindedness
- Openness
- Optimism
- Order
- Organization
- Originality
- Outlandishness
- Outrageousness
- Passion
- Peace
- Perceptiveness
- Perfection
- Perkiness
- Perseverance
- Persistence
- Persuasiveness
- Philanthropy
- Piety
- Playfulness
- Pleasantness
- Pleasure
- Poise
- Polish
- Popularity
- Potency
- Power
- Practicality
- Pragmatism
- Precision
- Preparedness

Presence
Privacy
Proactivity
Professionalism
Prosperity
Prudence
Punctuality
Purity
Realism
Reason
Reasonableness
Recognition
Recreation
Refinement
Reflection
Relaxation
Reliability
Religiousness
Resilience
Resolution
Resolve
Resourcefulness
Respect
Rest
Restraint
Reverence
Richness
Rigor
Sacredness
Sacrifice

Sagacity
Saintliness
Sanguinity
Satisfaction
Security
Self-control
Selflessness
Self-reliance
Sensitivity
Sensuality
Serenity
Service
Sexuality
Sharing
Shrewdness
Significance
Silence
Silliness
Simplicity
Sincerity
Skillfulness
Solidarity
Solitude
Soundness
Speed
Spirit
Spirituality
Spontaneity
Spunk
Stability

Stealth
Stillness
Strength
Structure
Success
Support
Supremacy
Surprise
Sympathy
Synergy
Teamwork
Temperance
Thankfulness
Thoroughness
Thoughtfulness
Thrift
Tidiness
Timeliness
Traditionalism
Tranquility
Transcendence
Trust
Trustworthiness
Truth
Understanding

Unflappability
Uniqueness
Unity
Usefulness
Utility
Valor
Variety
Victory
Vigor
Virtue
Vision
Vitality
Vivacity
Warmth
Watchfulness
Wealth
Willfulness
Willingness
Winning
Wisdom
Wittiness
Wonder
Youthfulness
Zeal

Bibliography

About Google. Retrieved December 12, 2019, from www.google.com/about

Block, C. (2020). *Chief Spartan Officer*. UAE: Passionpreneur Publishing.

Carnegie, D. (2009). *How to Win Friends and Influence People*. Simon & Schuster.

Constitution of United States (1776)

Collins, J. C., & Porras, J. I. (1991). Organizational Vision and Visionary Organizations. *California Management Review, 34*(1), 30-52.

Doran, G. T. (1981). There's a S.M.A.R.T. Way to Write Management's Goals and Objectives. *Management Review, 70*(11).

Drucker, P. F., & Collins, J. (2008). *The Five Most Important Questions You Will Ever Ask About Your Organization*. New York: Leader to Leader Institute.

Erickson, T. Meaning Is the New Money. Retrieved December 15, 2019, from https://hbr.org/2011/03/challenging-our-deeply-held-as

Feedback. (1994). *New Scientist,* (November 5).

García, H., Miralles, F., & Cleary, H. (2018). *Ikigai: The Japanese Secret to a Long and Happy Life*. Waterville, ME: Thorndike Press Large Print.

Gladwell, M. (2011). *Outliers: The Story of Success*. New York: Back Bay Books.

Hamwi, M. (2019). *Live Passionately: The Blueprint to Design a Life Truly Worth Living*. Melbourne, VC, Australia: Passionpreneur Publishing.

Haughey, D. (2014). A Brief History of SMART Goals. Retrieved January 2, 2020, from https://www.projectsmart.co.uk/brief-history-of-smart-goals.php

Holy Qu'ran

Hu, J., & Hirsh, J. B. (2017). Accepting Lower Salaries for Meaningful Work. *Frontiers in Psychology, 8*.

Law, T. (2018, April 05). How Ikigai can be applied to early-stage companies. Retrieved from https://wearehowdoi.com/news/2018/6/1/how-ikigai-can-be-applied-to-early-stage-companies

Malphurs, A. (1996). *Values-driven Leadership: Discovering and Developing Your Core Values for ministry*. Grand Rapids, Michigan: Baker Books.

Maxwell, J. C. (2011). *Beyond Talent: Become Someone Who Gets Extraordinary Results*. Thomas Nelson.

Mintzberg, H. (1994). *Rise and Fall of Strategic Planning*. Simon & Schuster.

Mossholder, K. W., Richardson, H. A., & Settoon, R. P. (2011). Human Resource Systems and Helping in Organizations: A Relational Perspective. *Academy of Management Review, 36*(1), 33-52.

Pearce, J. A., & David, F. (1987). Corporate Mission Statements: The Bottom Line. *Academy of Management Perspectives, 1*(2), 109-115.

Pinker, S. (2011). *The Better Angels of Our Nature: Why Violence Has Declined*. New York: Viking.

Robb, A., If Your Name Is Dennis, You're More Likely to Become a Dentist. Retrieved December 1, 2019, from https://newrepublic.com/article/116140/psychologists-say-our-names-affect-what-careers-we-choose

Sinek, S. Simon Sinek Goals – 2018 [Video file]. (2018) Retrieved December 20, 2019, from https://www.youtube.com/watch?v=m29q4Yh4U_0

Sinek, S. Values are Verbs – 2019 [Video file]. (2019) Retrieved December 22, 2019, from https://www.youtube.com/watch?v=o3Va_Y4cDSg

Sinek, S. (2017). *Find Your Why: A Practical Guide for Discovering Purpose for You and Your Team*. Penguin Books.

Sydney Rowing Club Handbook. (n.d.). Retrieved December 15, 2019, from https://www.sydneyrowingclub.com.au/wp-content/uploads/2019/11/Sydney-Rowing-Club-Handbook-Rev-4.5-22-October-2019.pdf

Universal Declaration of Human Rights. (n.d.). Retrieved December 10, 2019, from https://www.un.org/en/universal-declaration-human-rights/.

Warren, R. (2002). *The Purpose-Driven Life: What on Earth Am I Here For?* Grand Rapids, Michigan: Zondervan.

Winfrey, O. (2019). *The Path Made Clear: Discovering Your Life's Direction and Purpose*. London: Melcher.

www.ingramcontent.com/pod-product-compliance
Lightning Source LLC
Chambersburg PA
CBHW052042280426
43661CB00085B/68